GOVERNMENT PROCEDURES AND OPERATIONS

FEDERAL USER FEES

DESIGN, COLLECTION, USE AND EVALUATION CONSIDERATIONS

GOVERNMENT PROCEDURES AND OPERATIONS

Additional books in this series can be found on Nova's website under the Series tab.

Additional e-books in this series can be found on Nova's website under the eBooks tab.

GOVERNMENT PROCEDURES AND OPERATIONS

FEDERAL USER FEES

DESIGN, COLLECTION, USE AND EVALUATION CONSIDERATIONS

NOAH R. MYERS
EDITOR

nova publishers
New York

Library of Congress Cataloging-in-Publication Data

ISBN: 978-1-63484-868-8

Published by Nova Science Publishers, Inc. † New York

CONTENTS

PREFACE

The federal government will need to make the most of its resources to meet the emerging challenges of the 21st century. As new priorities emerge, policymakers have demonstrated interest in user fees as a means of financing new and existing services. User fees can be designed to reduce the burden on taxpayers to finance the portions of activities that provide benefits to identifiable users above and beyond what is normally provided to the public. By charging the costs of those programs or activities to beneficiaries, user fees can also promote economic efficiency and equity. However, to achieve these goals, user fees must be well designed. This book examines how the four key design and implementation characteristics of user fees—how fees are set, collected, used, and reviewed—may affect the economic efficiency, equity, revenue adequacy, and administrative burden of cost-based fees.

In: Federal User Fees
Editor: Noah R. Myers
ISBN: 978-1-63484-868-8

Chapter 1

FEDERAL USER FEES: A DESIGN GUIDE*

United States Government Accountability Office

WHY GAO DID THIS STUDY

The federal government will need to make the most of its resources to meet the emerging challenges of the 21st century. As new priorities emerge, policymakers have demonstrated interest in user fees as a means of financing new and existing services. User fees can be designed to reduce the burden on taxpayers to finance the portions of activities that provide benefits to identifiable users above and beyond what is normally provided to the public. By charging the costs of those programs or activities to beneficiaries, user fees can also promote economic efficiency and equity. However, to achieve these goals, user fees must be well designed.

GAO was asked to study how user fee design characteristics may influence the effectiveness of user fees. Specifically, GAO examined how the four key design and implementation characteristics of user fees—how fees are set, collected, used, and reviewed— may affect the economic efficiency, equity, revenue adequacy, and administrative burden of cost-based fees. GAO reviewed economic and policy literature on federal and nonfederal user fees, including prior GAO work, and used relevant case examples to illustrate different types of design elements and the impacts they may have.

---

* This is an edited, reformatted and augmented version of the United States Government Accountability Office publication, GAO-08-386SP, dated May 2008.

What GAO Found

Setting user fees: Setting user fees according to the beneficiary-pays principle can promote equity and economic efficiency. For cost-based fees, the extent to which a program provides benefits to the general public versus users and the cost of providing those benefits should, theoretically, guide how much of total program costs are paid for by user fees and the amount each user pays. Although this principle provides a useful guideline for setting fees, strictly following the principle is not always desirable or practical.

Collecting user fees: The primary challenge of determining when and how to collect a fee is striking a balance between ensuring compliance and minimizing administrative costs. In some cases, the collection systems of another agency or a nonfederal entity, such as a private sector enterprise, may be leveraged, as when the airlines collect passenger inspection fees.

Using user fees: Determining how fees will be used is a balancing act between Congressional oversight and agency flexibility. Congress gives agencies various degrees of access to collected fees. For example, fees may be dedicated to the related program or may instead be deposited to the general fund of the U.S. Treasury and not used specifically for the related program or agency. In addition, fee collections may be subject to appropriation or obligation limits, which increase opportunity for oversight but may limit agencies' ability to quickly respond to changing conditions.

Reviewing user fees: Agencies must substantively review their fees on a regular basis to ensure that they, Congress, and stakeholders have complete information. Reviews provide information on whether the fee rates and authorized activities are aligned with actual program costs and activities, may provide opportunities for stakeholder input, and can help promote understanding and acceptance of the fee.

Abbreviations

AMS	Agricultural Marketing Services
APHIS	Animal and Plant Health Inspection Service
AQI	Agricultural Quarantine Inspection
BLM	Bureau of Land Management
CBP	U.S. Customs and Border Protection
CFO	chief financial officer

Corps	U.S. Army Corps of Engineers
DHS	Department of Homeland Security
FAA	Federal Aviation Administration
FDA	Food and Drug Administration
GDP	gross domestic product
HMF	Harbor Maintenance Fee
HMTF	Harbor Maintenance Trust Fund
IOAA	Independent Offices Appropriation Act of 1952
MOE	maintenance of effort
MPF	Merchandise Processing Fee
NPS	National Park Service
OIC	Offer in Compromise
OMB	Office of Management and Budget
PAYGO	pay-as-you-go
PDUFA	Prescription Drug User Fee Act
REA	Federal Lands Recreation Enhancement Act
USCIS	U.S. Citizenship and Immigration Services
USDA	U.S. Department of Agriculture

* * *

May 29, 2008

Congressional Requesters

The federal government will need to make the most of its resources to meet the emerging challenges of the 21st century. As the nation continues to change in fundamental ways, a wide range of needs and demands have emerged, for example, evolving defense and homeland security programs, increasing global interdependence, and advances in science and technology. At the same time, our current long-term simulations of the federal budget show ever-larger deficits. As funds become increasingly scarce and new priorities emerge, policymakers have demonstrated interest in user fees as a means of financing new and existing services.

Total federal user fees are in the hundreds of billions of dollars annually and growing. According to Office of Management and Budget (OMB) data, total fee collections increased 69 percent from $138 billion in fiscal year 1999 to $233 billion in fiscal year 2007.[1] Even after adjusting for inflation, fee collections grew 39 percent. During this time period, total user fee collections varied from 6.4 to 7.6 percent of total federal spending (gross outlays).

User fees can be designed to reduce the burden on taxpayers to finance the portions of activities that provide benefits to identifiable users above and beyond what is normally provided to the public. By charging the costs of programs or activities to identifiable beneficiaries, user fees can promote economic efficiency and equity just as prices for private goods and services can do in a free and competitive private market. However, to achieve these goals, user fees must be well designed. You asked us to study how user fee design characteristics may influence the effectiveness of user fees. Specifically, we examined how the four key design and implementation characteristics of user fees—how fees are (1) set, (2) collected, (3) used, and (4) reviewed—may affect the economic efficiency, equity, revenue adequacy, and administrative burden of the fees.

There are various ways to design user fees to encourage greater efficiency, equity, and revenue adequacy and reduce the administrative burden on the agency and payers of the fees. We examined fees using criteria that have often been used to assess user fees and other government collections, specifically taxes.[2]

- **Efficiency:** By requiring identifiable beneficiaries to pay for the costs of services, user fees can simultaneously constrain demand and reveal the value that beneficiaries place on the service. If those benefiting from a service do not bear the full social cost of the service, they may seek to have the government provide more of the service than is economically efficient. User fees may also foster production efficiency by increasing awareness of the costs of publicly provided services and therefore increasing incentives to reduce costs where possible.
- **Equity:** Equity means that everyone pays their fair share, but the definition of fair share can have multiple facets, in part because beneficiaries and users may not be the same as discussed in the section "Setting User Fees." Under the beneficiary-pays principle, the beneficiaries of a service pay for the cost of providing the service from which they benefit. Under the ability-to-pay principle, those who are more capable of bearing the burden of fees should pay more for the service than those with less ability to pay.
- **Revenue adequacy:** Revenue adequacy is the extent to which the fee collections cover the intended share of costs. It encompasses the

extent to which collections may change over time relative to the cost of the program. For the purposes of our work, revenue adequacy also incorporates the concept of revenue stability, which generally refers to the degree to which short-term fluctuations in economic activity and other factors affect the level of fee collections.

- **Administrative burden:** This is the cost of administering the fee, including the cost of collection and enforcement, as well as the compliance burden (the administrative costs imposed on the payers of the fee).

These criteria interact and are often in conflict with each other; as such, there are tradeoffs to consider among the criteria when designing a fee. Every fee design will have pluses and minuses, and no design will satisfy everyone on all dimensions. The weight that different policymakers may place on different criteria will vary, depending on how they value different attributes. To that end, understanding the tradeoffs associated with different aspects of a fee's design can provide decision makers with better information and support more robust deliberations about user fee financing. The criteria, questions, and illustrative examples presented in this guide are designed to aid policymakers in thinking about issues to consider when designing new user fees and redesigning or updating existing fees.

The questions and tradeoffs discussed in this guide relate to cost-based user fees—including some dedicated excise taxes (i.e., those that have a "user pays" aspect to them, such as the federal gas tax)—for which private beneficiaries are discernable. They generally fall into two broad categories: (1) business-type transactions, such as recreation fees for parks and fees for grazing on federal land and (2) regulatory transactions, such as food inspection and immigration fees and fees for regulating the nuclear energy industry. Certain types of fees have particular design elements, such as setting market-based fee rates or insurance premiums, which are outside the scope of this review.

To address our objectives, we reviewed economic and policy literature on federal and nonfederal user fees, including our prior work on user fees. To illustrate different types of design elements and the impacts they may have, we used relevant case examples found in the literature, including our past reviews of user fees, in particular our recent reviews of the Department of Homeland Security's (DHS) U.S. Customs and Border Protection (CBP), U.S. Army Corps of Engineers (Corps), and U.S. Department of Agriculture (USDA) fees. We used data on total federal user fees and gross outlays for fiscal years 1999 through 2007 presented in OMB's *Analytical Perspectives* and adjusted those figures for inflation using a fiscal year, chain-weighted gross domestic product (GDP) price index.[3]

We performed our work from February 2007 through May 2008 in Washington, D.C. and Boston, Massachusetts.

BACKGROUND

User financing—in the form of user fees, user charges, or excise taxes on certain products—is one approach to financing federal programs or activities. User fees assign part or all of the costs of these programs and activities—the cost of providing a benefit that is above and beyond what is normally available to the general public—to readily identifiable users of those programs and activities. Because user fees represent a charge for a service or benefit received from a government program, payers may expect a tight link between their payments and the cost of providing services and have expectations about the quality of the related service.

Definition of User Fees

For the purposes of this guide we use the term user fees to include user fees as well as excise taxes with a "user pays" element.[4] Examples include those imposed on motor fuels, tires, and heavy vehicles that accrue to the Highway Trust Fund, from which Congress appropriates funds for federal highway and transit programs. Similarly, Federal Aviation Administration (FAA) activities are funded in part by excise taxes assessed on airline tickets, aviation fuel, and certain cargo.[5] A highway toll may also be considered a user fee because it is related to the specific use of a particular section of highway. The boundaries between fees and taxes are not always clear and the tradeoffs among design elements presented in this guide can be relevant to both.

In general, a user fee is related to some voluntary transaction or request for government goods or services above and beyond what is normally available to the public, such as a request that a public agency permit an applicant to practice law or medicine or construct a house or run a broadcast station.[6] Taxes, on the other hand, arise from the government's sovereign power to raise revenue and need not be related to any specific benefit, and payment is not optional; when Congress imposes taxes, it need not consider benefits bestowed by the government on an individual but may base taxation solely on an individual's ability to pay. The Supreme Court has ruled that a tax is "an enforced contribution to provide for the support of government."[7] The legal distinction between a "fee" and a "tax" can be complicated and depends largely on the context of the particular assessment. Whether a particular assessment is statutorily referred to as a tax or a fee is never legally determinative. Instead, federal courts will examine the structure and the context of the assessment's application.

Fees vary in the degree to which they can be considered truly voluntary because the availability of reasonable substitutes varies. For example, to enter certain national parks, one must pay an entrance fee. The fee is voluntary to the extent that there are alternatives to national parks for outdoor recreation, for example, state, county, or private parks and recreation facilities. In contrast, people who want to operate radio stations have no similarly close alternative and must obtain a license from the Federal Communications Commission and pay a fee for that license.

Authority to Charge Fees

Agencies derive their authority to charge fees either from the Independent Offices Appropriation Act of 1952 (IOAA)[8] or from specific statutory authority. IOAA provides broad authority to assess user fees or charges on identifiable beneficiaries by administrative regulation. User fees assessed under IOAA authority must be (1) fair and (2) based on costs to the government, the value of the service or thing to the recipient, public policy or interest serviced, and other relevant facts. Fees collected under this authority are deposited in the general fund of the U.S. Treasury and are generally not available to the agency or the activity generating the fees. Unless otherwise authorized by law, IOAA requires that agency regulations establishing a user fee are subject to policies prescribed by the President. OMB provides such guidance to executive branch agencies under this authority through Circular No. A-25.[9] The Circular establishes federal guidelines regarding user fees assessed under the authority of IOAA and other statutes, including the scope and types of activities subject to user fees and the basis upon which the fees are set. It also provides guidance for executive branch agency implementation of fees and the disposition of collections.[10]

In many instances, Congress has provided specific authority to federal agencies to assess user fees—in agency authorizing or appropriations legislation, for example. Legislation authorizing a user fee may enact a specified rate or amount to be assessed or may stipulate how the fee is to be calculated, such as a formula; the method and timing of collection; and the authorized uses of the fee collections, which may be broadly or narrowly defined. The amount of a fee may be set to partially or fully recover costs or may be set according to some other basis (e.g., market value). Specific authorizing statutes may even grant the agency broad discretion to set and revise fee rates without Congressional approval—that is, solely through the regulatory process—based on various factors. Specific user fee statutes should be construed consistent with IOAA and OMB Circular No. A-25 to the extent possible as part of an overall statutory scheme.[11]

SETTING USER FEES: DETERMINING BENEFICIARIES AND ALLOCATING COSTS

Of the four components of implementing a user fee, setting the rate of the fee is perhaps the most challenging because determining the cost of the service is often quite complex and requires consideration of a range of issues (see figure 1).

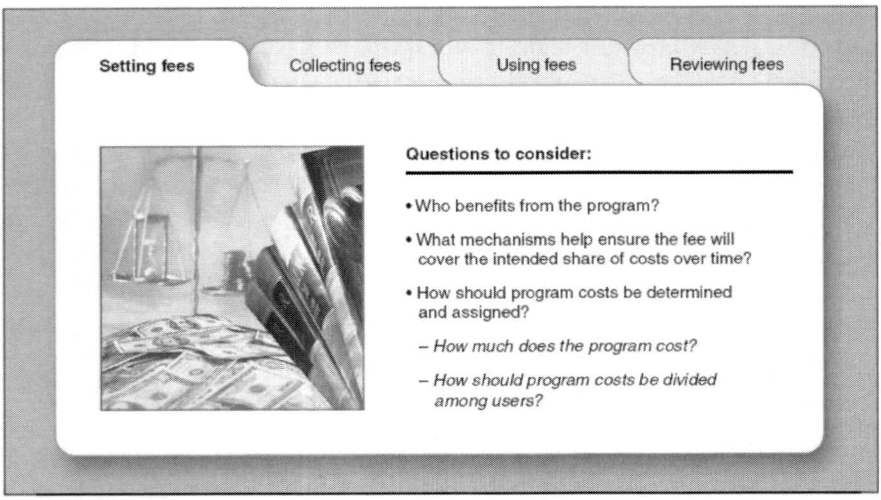

Sources: GAO (information); PhotoDisc and Comstock © (images).

Figure 1. Questions to Consider When Setting User Fees.

To What Extent does the Program Benefit both the General Public and Users?

In theory, the extent to which a program is funded by user fees should generally be guided by who primarily benefits from the program, though, as we discuss later, the extent to which a program benefits users or the general public is not usually clear cut. This is known as the beneficiary- pays principle. Under this principle, if a program primarily benefits the general public (e.g., national defense), it should be supported by general revenue, not user fees; if a program primarily benefits identifiable users, such as customers of the U.S. Postal Service, it should be funded by fees; and if a program benefits both the general public and users, it should be funded in part by fees and in part by general revenues.[12] As shown in figure 2, the beneficiary-pays principle can promote equity by assigning costs to those who both use and benefit from the services. First, as shown on the left side of figure 2, the extent to which a program provides benefits to the general public versus users should guide the proportion of total program costs that are paid for by general revenues versus user fees. Second, as shown on the right side of the illustration, the cost of providing the benefits to each user should be determined and assigned through user fees. Figure 3 depicts selected federal programs funded according to this principle.

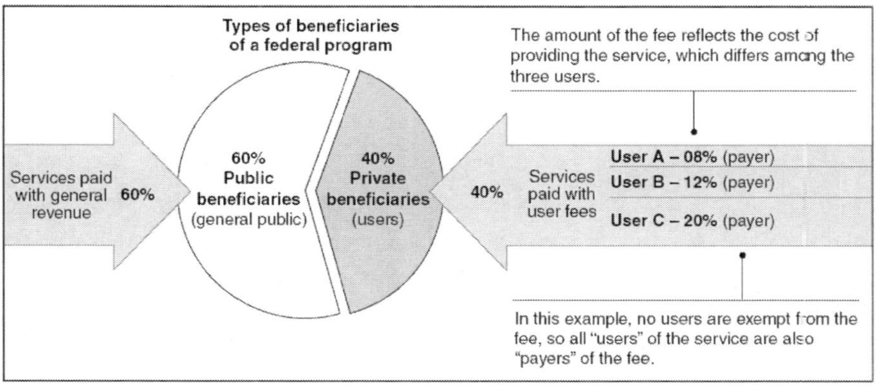

Source: GAO.

Note: Though not shown in this example, fees may include exemptions, so that some "users" of the program are not "payers" of the fee. The cost of providing the service to exempt users may be paid for with general revenues or by the fees of other users.

Figure 2. Simplified, Hypothetical Example of Assigning Program Costs to Beneficiaries, Including Users.

National defense

National defense benefits the general public. Therefore, it is fully supported by general revenues, rather than user fees.

FDA prescription drug reviews

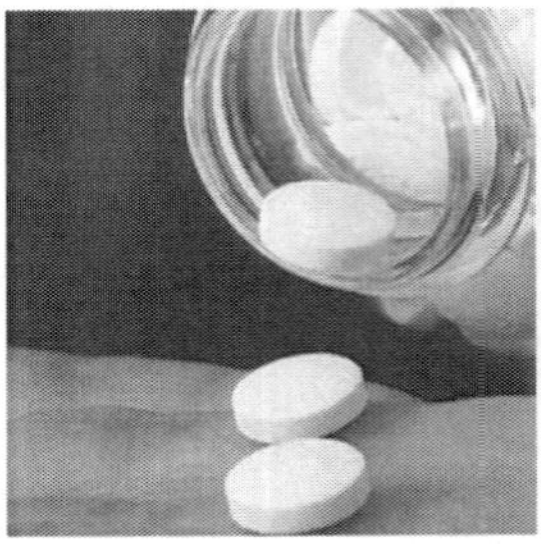

FDA prescription drug reviews benefit drug sponsors and the public. Therefore, they are supported in part by general revenues and in part by user fees.

U.S. Postal Service

Postal services directly benefit users sending letters or other mail. Therefore, they are almost fully supported by user fees, rather than general revenues.[a]

Sources: GAO (information); images: PhotoDisc (right and left), Dynamic Graphics (center).

[a] The U.S. Postal Service gets a small proportion of its funding from general revenues for costs of providing free mail for the blind and overseas voting.

Figure 3. Examples of Federal Programs with Different Levels of Funding from User Fees.

Secondary beneficiaries of a program generally are not considered in this examination. For example, consumers of new prescription drugs are secondary beneficiaries of prescription drug reviews, which provide a primary benefit to the drug sponsors.[13] Similarly, fees should be charged to the direct user, even if that payer then passes the cost of the fee on to others. The entities that bear the burden of a fee—what economists call the incidence of the fee—are not necessarily those who legally must pay the fee. Fees may be passed along to others through price changes, as the fee may change the price of one good relative to another and therefore affect the allocation of resources. How prices change—and therefore the incidence of the fee—depends on (1) how responsive market supply and demand are to price changes (price elasticity) and (2) market conditions that affect an entity's ability to control prices.[14] The ability of payers to pass along the fee does not necessarily change the economic efficiency effects of the fee but can affect its perceived equity and the transparency of the fee.[15]

User fees set under the beneficiary-pays principle can also enhance economic efficiency by ensuring that resources are allocated to the most highly valued use, as users make adjustments to their consumption of the service based on their costs and benefits. For example, setting a Food and Drug Administration (FDA) fee for new prescription drug applications too high could discourage the development of new drugs. On the other hand, setting the fee too low induces overuse of agency resources and services. To the extent a fee is voluntary, user fees based on a program or service's total costs may also act as a market test and can help ensure that the benefits of the program are at least as great as its costs.

Under the beneficiary-pays principle, the government may wish to charge some users a lower fee or no fee to encourage certain behaviors that provide a public benefit, such as advancing a public policy goal (e.g., promoting free trade). For example:

- Potential profits from the development of "orphan" drugs—those that treat rare diseases—are limited by the small size of their market, and therefore drug companies may be reluctant to invest in them; such drugs are exempt from the FDA prescription drug application fee to encourage their development.
- Imports from certain least developed countries are exempt from CBP's Merchandise Processing Fee (MPF), which both addresses their ability to pay and may help promote their economic development. DHS officials noted that in other cases MPF exemptions have been used as a tool to negotiate free trade agreements; an exemption may be extended as a concession for the reduction of import tariffs on certain U.S. goods.
- Low-income taxpayers are exempt from the $150 application fee for the Internal Revenue Service's Offer in Compromise (OIC) program—a program for taxpayers unable to fully pay their tax liabilities—to make the program more accessible and encourage participation.

Although user fees can promote one facet of equity—the beneficiary-pays principle—they may run contrary to another facet—the ability-to-pay principle. To the extent that user fees are a substitute for funding through general tax revenues, they may be less progressive than taxes and therefore shift additional burden on those less able to pay. Fees (or taxes) that are proportionally more burdensome for low-income than high- income individuals are said to be regressive. To address this concern, the design of a fee may consider the ability of a user to pay, for example, by exempting low-income users or scaling fees by some measure of ability to pay.

In certain cases user fees may not be the most equitable, efficient option for funding a program. Examples include fees for

- government programs intended to provide a benefit based on need or merit, such as the Department of Housing and Urban Development's Section 8 housing voucher program (which assists low-income families, including the elderly and the disabled);
- competing sectors within an industry (e.g., modes of transportation) if the other sectors are not subject to similar fees; and
- new industries that face high initial costs and may need government support until they can become self-sustaining.

Abrupt imposition of new or substantially increased user fees could have unintended consequences. For example, in May 2007, U.S. Citizenship and Immigration Services (USCIS) published a new fee schedule that raised fees effective July 2007 for immigrant and naturalization benefit applications by an average of 88 percent. Large numbers of applicants filed for benefits before the increase took effect, which contributed to a surge that exacerbated USCIS's backlog of applications. In cases like this, transitional measures such as grandfather clauses or phasing in increases might help address concerns about the adverse effects of the abrupt imposition of a fee, while implementing the beneficiary-pays principle gradually. However, as is the case with exemptions, the benefits of transitional measures must be balanced with the likelihood of reduced efficiency and equity gains and increased administrative costs. Furthermore, delaying a fee increase may also have adverse effects on an agency's operations. In some cases, new or increased user fees may also cause decreases in the value of privately owned assets. We have previously reported on how user fees can result in such capital losses, as well as ways of determining when, how much, and to whom compensation for these losses should be paid.[16]

Although the beneficiary-pays principle is a useful guideline for assigning costs, determining a program's beneficiaries and the extent to which a program benefits users, the general public, or both is not usually clear cut. For example, in prior work we found that National Park Service (NPS) staff reported that they did not want to raise federal grazing fees assessed on ranchers, even though these fees were lower than fees charged by other government agencies and private landowners, in part because grazing not only benefits ranchers but also benefits parks—for example, by controlling vegetation.[17] In another example, USDA food safety inspections benefit the meat and poultry industries as well as the general public: inspections improve consumer confidence in the safety of those food products and the companies can advertise their products as USDA inspected, which may enhance the perceived quality. The inspections also benefit the general public by preventing the spread of communicable diseases carried by meat and poultry products, but it is difficult to quantify that public health benefit and consequently the extent to which the program should be covered by user fees versus general revenues.

Fees can be practical, equitable, and efficient only when the users can be identified and charged for the service or program. Sometimes, however, it may be difficult to identify specific users or to collect fees from them, making it difficult to follow the beneficiary-pays principle. NPS, which can identify and verify some users, also collects fees from air tour operators that fly over certain national park units. However, in prior work we found that because NPS could not verify air tour activity over the parks, it relied on operators to voluntarily report their air tours and pay the required fees.[18] Some tour operators paid and some did not, resulting in inequities and less-than-owed fee collections.

What Mechanisms Help Ensure the Fee Will Cover the Intended Share of Costs Over Time?

Fee collections should be sufficient to cover the intended portion of program costs over time. Although the costs of any particular program may rise or fall, there is a general concern that fees may not keep pace with increases in costs because of factors such as inflation. For example, in recent testimony we noted that revenues to support federal highway and transit funding are eroding in part because the federal motor fuel tax, which is set at the fixed amount of 18.4 cents per gallon, has not been increased since 1993. Therefore, the purchasing power of fuel tax revenues has eroded.[19] To address these concerns, OMB Circular No. A-25 directs agencies to set fees as percentages of some appropriate base rather than fixed dollar amounts whenever possible. However, fees set at a percentage rate of some value (the basis) will not remain aligned with program costs if the value of the basis does not rise and fall in line with changes in the program costs. For example, in recent years the Harbor Maintenance Fee (HMF), which is assessed at a rate of 0.125 percent of the value of commercial cargo, has resulted in substantially higher collections than spending because the growth in the volume and value of commercial cargo has exceeded increases in harbor maintenance spending.

As a result, HMF collections exceeded expenditures by over $506 million in fiscal year 2007. Thus, regardless of whether a fee is set at a flat dollar amount or a percentage rate, regular reviews and updates of the fee are necessary to ensure that the fee remains aligned with program costs (see final section of this guide, "Reviewing User Fees: Providing Information on Costs and Program Activities and Facilitating Stakeholder Support").

On the other hand, fee payers and other stakeholders may be concerned that, over time, the portion of program costs covered by general revenues will decline. This concern may be well founded; in prior work on fee- reliant agencies, we found that increased user fee collections sometimes appeared to have replaced appropriated funds.[20] This substitution can be a particular concern when new or increased fees are assessed to augment total funding for a service or program. For example, part of the rationale for FDA's Prescription Drug User Fee Act (PDUFA) fees was to increase FDA resources for—thereby decreasing the processing time of—new drug applications. To assuage fee payers' concerns that fees might not be used to increase the level of an existing service—but instead simply be used as a substitute for funding from general revenues—a fee statute may provide a kind of maintenance of effort (MOE) requirement in terms of general revenues funding.[21] For example, in any year, FDA may only collect and spend PDUFA fees when Congress has appropriated from general revenues a certain amount specifically for FDA new drug application reviews.[22] Such provisions, however, can have unintended consequences. In prior work we reported that according to FDA officials the spending baseline for the drug review program reduced available resources for other activities, such as reviewing over-the-counter and generic products and inspecting medical product manufacturing facilities.[23] Increased reliance on fees as a source of funding may lead to a misalignment between the beneficiaries of a program and the sources of funding for the program and can have significant implications for agencies.

How Should Program Costs be Determined and Assigned to Users?

Assigning costs requires (1) determining how much a program costs and (2) determining how to assign program costs among different users. As the beneficiary-pays principle is useful in guiding decisions about how program costs are divided between the general public and users, it can also guide how program costs are assigned among users. Basing fees on the cost of providing the program or service from which a user benefits enhances equity, as measured by the beneficiary-pays principle, as each user pays for the cost of services actually used. As discussed above, fees set following the beneficiary-pays principle also generally promote economic efficiency, as users take into account the "price" of a service when deciding how much of the service to consume.

How Much does the Program Cost?

To set fees so that total collections cover the intended share of program costs, a reliable accounting of total program cost is important.[24] To obtain such an accounting, it is necessary to determine which activities and costs should be included and which should not.[25] Unless the authorizing legislation specifies costs that should be included or excluded, agencies should follow OMB guidance. OMB Circulars No. A-25 and No. A-11 instruct agencies to include all direct and indirect costs when determining full cost, including but not limited to personnel costs, including salaries and benefits such as medical insurance and retirement; physical overhead; consulting; material and supply costs; utilities; insurance; travel; rents or imputed rents on land, buildings, and equipment; management and supervisory costs; costs of collecting and enforcing fees; research; establishment of standards and regulation; and imputed costs.[26] In prior work we found inconsistent implementation of this guidance. Some fees designed to cover the full cost of a program include all direct and indirect costs, but others do not. The power marketing administrations, for example, include all direct and indirect costs—including the cost of employee retirement benefits paid by the Office of Personnel Management—when setting their electricity rates.[27] On the other hand, in recent work, we found that USDA's Animal and Plant Health Inspection Service (APHIS) did not include certain indirect and imputed costs when calculating the Agricultural Quarantine Inspection (AQI) fee rate.[28]

Fees should also be set and adjusted to cover the intended share of costs over time, which means agencies must project and consider future program costs. For example, in 2006 USDA's Food Safety and Inspection Service set fee rates through fiscal year 2008 for its meat, poultry, and egg products overtime inspection services. The fee rates for each year included adjustments for inflation and employee pay raises, so that future fee collections were projected to grow with program costs.[29] When more than one agency implements—and therefore incurs costs related to—a fee program, those agencies should work together to agree on a method for estimating future costs and collections. APHIS and CBP, for example, used different forecasting assumptions related to the AQI fees. In response to our recent work, the agencies now use common assumptions.[30]

Whether fee rates will be set using average cost or marginal cost is also an important consideration when setting fees. Setting fees at a rate equal to the marginal cost of providing the service or product to the user maximizes economic efficiency.[31] In part because it is often difficult to measure marginal cost, fee rates are sometimes set based on average cost. The AQI fees are intended to cover total program costs; to set these fees, APHIS projects program costs for different inspection types (e.g., air passenger, commercial aircraft, and commercial vessels) and divides each by the total projected number of each type of payer. That is, each airline pays the same fee per arrival to cover the costs related to inspecting aircraft.

When marginal costs are measurable but are low relative to the fixed costs of the program, setting the fee at marginal cost will lead to collections less than total costs. In these cases, users may be charged more than marginal costs or the program may be funded in part through general revenues.[32] One option is to create a two-part fee consisting of (1) a flat fee to cover fixed costs and (2) a usage-based fee to cover marginal costs. For example, the marginal cost of providing electricity (i.e., operating power plants and maintaining transmission lines) is small compared with the costs of building power plants and transmission lines; thus, electricity consumers could be charged a flat monthly charge plus a charge that would vary based on their consumption.[33]

If a fee is to recover the costs associated with an agency program or service or some portion thereof, it is critical that agencies record, accumulate, and analyze timely and reliable data relating to those costs, consistent with applicable accounting standards.[34] Many agencies, however, lack reliable cost data.[35] For example, we previously reported that DHS's U.S. Immigrations and Customs Enforcement lacked adequate cost data to determine the portion of costs related to international air passenger immigration inspections, a fee-funded activity.[36] Because generating and maintaining reliable cost data can be expensive, agencies must consider the costs of implementing, maintaining, and using financial management systems when determining the level of cost detail they need. Recognizing this, OMB Circular No. A-25 notes that program cost should be determined or estimated from the best available records of the agency and that new cost accounting systems need not be established solely for this purpose. Still, unreliable cost information can skew fee-setting decisions, so management needs reliable cost information to ensure that user fees recover the intended share of costs. As such, each agency should determine the appropriate level of detail for its cost accounting processes and procedures.

How should Program Costs be Allocated across Users?

If the cost of providing a service varies for different types of users, the fee may vary (a user-specific fee) or be set at an average rate (a systemwide fee). All other things being equal, user-specific fees promote equity and economic efficiency because the amount of the fee is closely aligned with the cost of the service.[37] Systemwide fees may be higher or lower than the actual cost of providing a service to certain types of users. As a result there may be cross-subsidies across users. For example, we recently reported that FAA's current funding structure raises concerns about equity and efficiency because users pay more or less than the costs of the air traffic control services they receive and therefore may lack incentives to use the national airspace system as efficiently as possible.[38] Because user-specific fees require agencies to track the costs of providing service to different users, these fees are often more costly to administer than systemwide fees. Fees charged to vessel operators for overtime immigration inspections are user specific. The fee is only assessed when the vessel operator or its agent requests an overtime inspection. The amount of the fee varies depending on the number and pay grade of the inspectors and the amount of time spent on the inspection. We recently reported that this structure increases the fee's administrative costs.[39] According to CBP estimates, the cost of processing and billing the fee was 26 percent of related collections in fiscal year 2007. In contrast, the commercial vessel AQI fee is a systemwide fee. Vessel owners/operators pay the $492 fee regardless of whether or not the ship is actually inspected by an agricultural specialist and regardless of the agricultural risk posed by the vessel. In managing these types of trade-offs between the benefits and drawbacks of user-specific versus systemwide fees, several factors may be important to consider.

1. **The purpose of a program:** Systemwide fees may promote a policy goal such as helping to support national systems. For example, despite variation in the amount of maintenance dredging needed at different ports, the HMF is imposed uniformly at all ports at which shipments are subject to the fee in order to support a national port system. This means that users of naturally deep draft ports that require little dredging (e.g., Seattle) in effect subsidize users of shallower and river ports (e.g., New Orleans). A user-specific fee may be more desirable

if the fee is seen as a way to support individual entities or locations or when maximizing economic efficiency outweighs the desire to support a national system through the imposition of a uniform fee.

2. **The amount of the fee:** If the fee is small relative to other costs that a user faces, it may be less important to have a user-specific fee with different rates. For example, several ships' agents we spoke with noted that carriers rarely question federal vessel inspection fees, in part because the fees are such a small part of a commercial vessel's overall expenses that they do not affect business decisions.
3. **The amount of cost variation among users:** If there are numerous different groups of users and a small cost variation among them, the efficiency gains of a user-specific fee may be overwhelmed by the added administrative costs. Conversely, if a program has a relatively small number of user groups and the cost of providing the service to those groups differs significantly, then user-specific fees might be both beneficial and feasible.

Some fees include provisions for exemptions, waivers, and caps to promote certain policy goals and these provisions affect how program costs are allocated among users. As discussed previously, exemptions can promote one kind of equity by factoring the users' ability to pay into the fee rate formula.[40] However, as with systemwide fees, such provisions may also increase cross-subsidies between users. Exemptions and caps may also raise equity and efficiency concerns. For example, shipments into certain ports are not subject to the HMF, which may make these ports less costly to use than ports that are subject to the HMF. Shippers may have an incentive to use a port that might otherwise not be the most cost-efficient port to use, so the HMF as designed may create competitive advantages and disadvantages among ports. Stakeholders at HMF ports argued that the exemption is inequitable and can diminish a port's ability to compete. For example, officials at the port of Boston told us that they believe that one importer moved its operations from Boston to the port of Quonset/Davisville in Rhode Island where shipments are not subject to the HMF to avoid paying the fee.[41] Similarly, officials from ports located near international borders reported that the HMF disadvantages them relative to nearby foreign ports. Seattle port authority officials consider the HMF to be a "punitive assessment" because they said it decreases Seattle's competitiveness against nearby Canadian ports (which do not charge the fee). The officials noted that the port of Vancouver actively promotes itself as not charging the HMF and said this partly explains why the port of Vancouver is growing faster than the Seattle port.

Reliably accounting for the costs and benefits associated with such provisions is important in order to ensure that these provisions are achieving the intended results. In fully-fee-funded programs, if some users are exempt from paying fees, total fee collections cannot cover total program costs unless other users pay a higher fee to cover the costs of the exempted users. For example, commercial and private vessels are both subject to agricultural quarantine inspections, but private vessels are exempt from the AQI fees. In prior work we found that the costs of these private vessel inspections are included in the AQI fee charged to commercial vessels. Thus commercial vessels are paying for the cost of inspecting private vessels. An alternative to cross-subsidization would be to pay for the costs of providing services to exempt entities through general revenues. In this way the policy goal is attained and the general public, rather than other users, make up the cost of exempt users or discounted fees.

Finally, like user-specific fees, fee exemptions and caps can increase administrative costs to the agency because the agency must carefully track when fees are due and from whom rather than simply charging everyone. Commercial vessel operators are generally assessed a $437 customs inspection fee when they arrive at port, but the fee is capped at $5,955 per calendar year. This is approximately 13.6 payments. This means that CBP has to calculate the point at which the vessel has reached the cap and is no longer subject to the fee. We recently reported that the cap increases CBP's administrative costs and the potential for errors.[42] This issue was particularly problematic in 2007 because a fee increase took effect on April 1, 2007, so vessels arriving before and after that date paid two different rates. Since the fee cap applies to payments received within a calendar year, it was even more difficult for CBP to calculate the total amount paid and determine if a vessel had reached the cap.

COLLECTING USER FEES: BALANCING COMPLIANCE WITH ADMINISTRATIVE COSTS

The primary challenge in determining when and how to collect a fee is striking a balance between ensuring compliance and minimizing administrative costs (see figure 4).

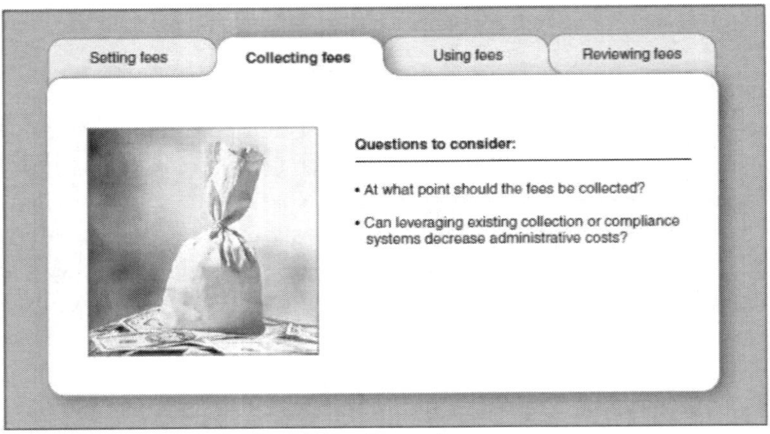

Sources: GAO (information); PhotoDisc (images).

Figure 4. Questions to Consider When Designing How User Fees Will Be Collected.

At What Point should the Fees be Collected?

Fees can be collected (1) at the point of sale before the service is provided, as airline passenger fees are paid when a ticket is purchased; (2) at the point of service, as when visitors enter a national park; or (3) after the service has been provided, for example when the agency bills the user for a service, as with overtime vessel inspections.[43] Collecting the fee at the point of sale or point of service may decrease administrative costs since billing becomes unnecessary. However, point-of-sale/point-of- service collections do not always ensure low administrative costs since other practices can considerably complicate a point-of-sale/service collections system. For example, commercial vessel customs inspection fees are collected by inspectors at the time of inspection, usually in the form of a check. We recently reported that because these collections are not automated, they are administratively costly. When an agency collects fees on the spot rather than billing for services (e.g., the national parks system), the agency may have less work to do in tracking who has paid and who has not, thus reducing administrative tasks associated with ensuring compliance. However, internal controls for fee collections are still necessary.

In some cases, collecting the fee at the point of service would present challenges that make doing so impractical. For example, if CBP collected fees from international air passengers at the airport, as is the practice in some other countries, inspection wait times for passengers would likely increase. For some fees, users are billed for services. This may create additional administrative costs since agency billings for services provided can add an extra step to the process. In some instances agencies are able to reduce their cost of collecting fees by using electronic payments or lockboxes[44] or enabling users to prepay their fees, thus reducing payments from many to perhaps one time per year. Commercial trucks entering the United States, for example, are subject to a $5.25 AQI fee, payable upon arrival. However, the owner or operator of the truck can prepay the AQI fee annually and receive a truck transponder that covers all entries for the calendar year, which enables CBP to inspect the truck and then wave the driver through, rather than taking the time to collect the fee at each crossing.[45] This prepayment reduces the administrative costs for both the agency, which may collect an annual payment instead of payments for every inspection, and the payer, who can make one payment per year rather than paying at each crossing.

Can Leveraging Existing Collections or Compliance Systems Decrease Administrative Costs?

In some cases, it makes sense for the agency to coordinate the collection or audit function with a third party. Specifically, when an entity or industry (e.g., shippers) is assessed multiple user fees there may be opportunities for one agency to collect on behalf of others. For example, HMF collections are used by the Corps for harbor operations and maintenance costs, but the fee is collected by CBP because CBP has the administrative structures in place to collect other fees and duties assessed on the value of imported goods. It is less costly for the government and payers of the fee for CBP to collect the fee as part of the formal entry process than it would be for the Corps or another entity to establish a new collections process. This cost saving occurs because CBP already values cargo for the assessment of duties so there is no duplication of effort. We recently reported that customs brokers with whom we spoke said that this system for collecting the HMF assessed on imported goods works well, is efficient, and imposes minimal administrative costs.[46] It may also make sense for agencies to coordinate fee collections when multiple federal agencies administer similar programs. For example, the Bureau of Land Management (BLM) manages grazing programs operated on both BLM and Department of Energy lands.[47] Similarly, consolidating the audit function of related fees within one agency or department can lessen the administrative costs of auditing them. For example, the audit function for the customs, immigration, and AQI user fee remittances by air carriers was consolidated under a memorandum of understanding between APHIS, the former U.S. Customs Service, and the former Immigration and Naturalization Service before the three related inspection functions were consolidated under CBP.[48] In some instances, as when CBP collects the HMF on behalf of the Corps, the agency is compensated for its cost of collecting the fee.[49]

In some cases, a nonfederal entity such as a state government or private sector enterprise has an existing infrastructure that can collect the fees. Passenger inspection fees, for example, are collected by airlines and cruise lines along with ticket fares; the collections are then remitted to CBP. However, when a private party takes over the collection function, ensuring compliance may become more complicated, contributing to administrative costs. Agencies may use audits to monitor and enforce compliance with the requirement to remit fees. CBP audits airlines and cruise lines to ensure that they are collecting and remitting the inspection fees as required. There are a range of other tools that can encourage compliance in these situations, for example, bond requirements and rewards and penalties. However, we have previously reported that to be effective, rewards and penalties must meet specific criteria, that is, they must provide optimal incentives and must correspond with performance.[50]

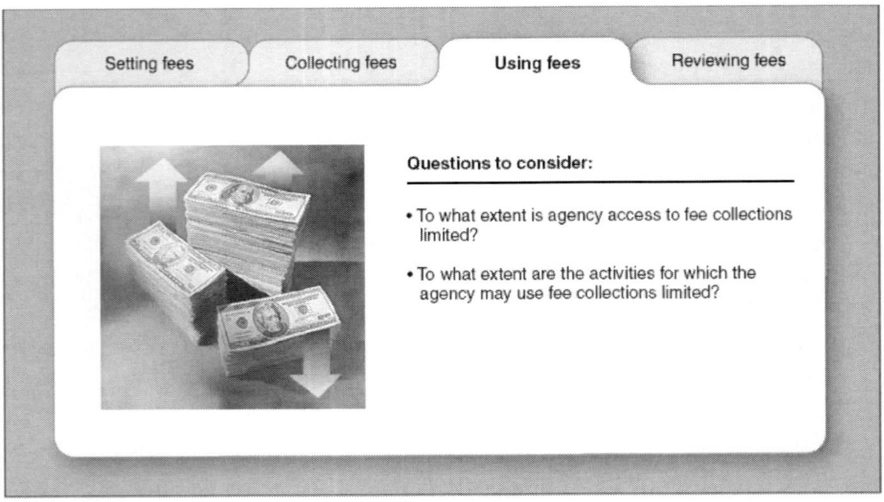

Sources: GAO (information); PhotoDisc (images).

Figure 5. Questions to Consider When Designing How User Fees Can Be Used.

USING USER FEES: BALANCING CONGRESSIONAL OVERSIGHT, AGENCY FLEXIBILITY, AND STAKEHOLDER EXPECTATIONS

Congress determines to what extent an agency may access (obligate and spend) fee collections. On the one hand, when the use of fee collections is not dedicated to the related program or agency, Congress has greater flexibility to make decisions about allocating resources and play an active oversight role.[51] While some maintain that the merits of a program, rather than its ability to generate fees, should influence federal funding decisions, dedicating fee collections to the program that generated the fee and giving the agency authority to obligate and expend the fees readily and decide how the collections will be used enhance the agency's flexibility and ability to respond quickly to changing conditions. Some have suggested that agencies will have less motivation to collect and users to pay if the fees are not credited to the activity that generated the fee. The extent to which this is the case is unclear. Further, this may be dealt with by engaging stakeholders—both in and out of government—to help improve their understanding of the purpose and design of the fee. In designing a fee, Congress has various mechanisms it can use to strike a balance between flexibility and oversight (see figure 5).

What are the Statutory Controls on Agency Use of Fee Collections?

Agency use of fee collections is determined by Congress. If fee collections must be annually appropriated to an agency before the agency may obligate and expend such collections, an agency has less independence in using them than fees that are permanently appropriated.[52] Requiring an appropriation increases opportunities for Congressional oversight on a regular basis. Expenditures from the Harbor Maintenance Trust Fund (HMTF), for example, are subject to annual appropriation, enabling Congress to annually determine the level of federal spending on harbor maintenance rather than automatically equating spending with total fee collections. Although the HMTF had a balance of almost $4 billion at the end of fiscal year 2007, the Corps obligated $798 million and $910 million from the fund in fiscal years 2006 and 2007, respectively.[53] The level of spending from the HMTF reflects Congressional priorities, possibly including reduction of the overall federal budget deficit.[54]

Some stakeholders said, however, that there is a backlog of harbor maintenance needs and that the misalignment between the amount of fee collections and expenditures undermines the credibility of the fee.[55]

Conversely, a fee may be designed to give the agency authority to use collections without additional Congressional action; this design may enable the agency to respond more quickly to customers or to changing conditions.[56] For example, the authorizing statute makes USDA Agricultural Marketing Services (AMS) fees directly available to the agency without further Congressional action. A 1999 USDA report on user fees noted that because AMS's services are voluntary and because the agency is financed largely through user fees, AMS has a strong incentive to develop services for which the industry is willing to pay. The report also asserts that if AMS did not retain these fees, innovations in service delivery would generate no financial return for the agency.[57] Further, the report stated that expanded agency discretion for the use of fee collections will have the greatest effect in agencies with substantial discretion for adjusting the types and amounts of services they provide. Creating a structure for oversight becomes even more important when agency discretion to use fee collections is expanded.

Permanent authority for fee collections also increases agency flexibility. With permanent authority, funds are available until expended, which enables agencies to carry forward unexpended collections to subsequent years and match fee collections to average program costs over more than 1 year. Such carryovers are one way agencies can establish reserve accounts, that is, revenue to sustain operations in the event of a sharp downturn in collections. For programs in which fees are expected to cover program costs and program costs do not necessarily decline with a drop in fee collections, a reserve is important. For example, the AQI fee statute gives APHIS permanent authority to use the collected fees and APHIS maintains a reserve in case of emergency. According to APHIS, the reserve is necessary because the AQI program is funded solely through user fee collections. However, with permanent spending authority, agencies may have less incentive to limit total collections to total costs.

Whether a fee program is designated as mandatory or discretionary within the budget context may affect the federal budget process more broadly.[58] Mandatory programs are subject to "pay-as-you-go" (PAYGO) rules if they are in effect.[59] Under such budget rules, increases in mandatory spending or decreases in revenue must be deficit neutral, that is, they must be offset by a decrease in mandatory spending or an increase in revenue. For example, if the rate of the HMF, which is classified as a mandatory governmental receipt, were reduced and total collections decreased, Congress would have to offset the lost revenues to comply with PAYGO rules. This requirement has in the past led to situations in which extensions of expiring fees are used to offset increases in unrelated programs.[60] Programs that are classified as discretionary are affected by applicable discretionary spending limits under the Concurrent Budget Resolution. Because some fees are classified as discretionary spending, they must be considered in discretionary spending calculations.[61]

Whether fees are designed so that collections are received directly or on a reimbursement basis also affects agency flexibility. The former offers the advantage of making funds immediately available to an agency, increasing its flexibility to plan and respond to changing conditions. The AQI fee collections are shared between CBP and APHIS, but only APHIS has authority to use its portion of the collections directly. According to APHIS, having the funds automatically available is useful because it facilitates the ability to keep pace with workload demands and respond quickly to unplanned needs. CBP's portion of the AQI fee collections—as well as its portion of the Immigration User Fee—is set up as a "reimbursable account," wherein the agency must spend other appropriations and apply for reimbursement. This design means it takes longer for CBP to get fee collections than for APHIS. According to CBP, this "reimbursable" arrangement results in less flexibility and a greater administrative burden.[62] Similarly, issues may occur when a program has large up-front costs (e.g., to develop an information technology system or purchase a capital asset). Fees collected over subsequent years to cover those costs would need to be either transferred to the U.S. Treasury's general fund or "saved" for future capital expenditures, depending on the statutory authority, because they cannot be used to reimburse appropriations made in a prior fiscal year.

How Broadly or Narrowly are the Authorized Uses of the Fee Collections Defined?

How broadly or narrowly Congress defines the authorized uses for the fee affects agency flexibility. For example, the AQI fee statute makes the fee collections available to cover the costs of providing agricultural quarantine inspection services and administrative costs related to the fee. The customs inspection fees, however, are only available to reimburse appropriations for a limited, prioritized set of activities.[63] Congress may also limit agency flexibility in the use of the fees by directing the agency to use the fees at the location where the fees were collected. NPS had a now- expired pilot program under which 80 percent of fee collections were retained and used by the park where they were collected.[64]

Statutes that narrowly limit how fees may be used could reduce Congress's and an agency's flexibility in making resource decisions[65] and reduce the agency's ability to adjust to changing priorities or program needs. The previously referenced NPS program is an example. We reported that restricting use of the 80 percent of fee collections from the NPS program to the sites at which they were collected created funding imbalances. This restriction resulted in some high-revenue sites having more revenue than needed to meet priority needs and contributed to a backlog of priority needs at lower-revenue sites.[66] Restrictions on use of fees may fail to keep pace with program needs over time as activities that support the service change. This can result in authorized activities that are misaligned with actual service or program activities. We recently reported, for example, that CBP officials said that since the terrorist attacks of September 11, 2001, the merchandise processing program has a greater focus on security than was the case in previous years. Although the increase is understandable, it has led to a situation in which activities associated with merchandise processing, including screening and inspecting conveyances and inspecting vessels and containers, are not reimbursable by the Merchandise Processing Fee (MPF), even though CBP views these activities as part of the merchandise processing service, the cost of which is offset by MPF collections.[67] Recalling the earlier discussion in this guide about public versus private benefits, if it is determined that a portion of merchandise processing activities primarily relates to national security—benefits that primarily accrue to the general public—a case could also be made that the corresponding costs be funded by general revenues.

Finally, although narrowing the authorized uses of a fee in statute may facilitate Congressional oversight, it can also increase agency administrative costs. Ensuring proper use of fee collections may require collecting more detailed cost data at a greater cost to the agency. For example, we recently reported that CBP must track the time CBP officers spend on authorized activities for several of its inspection fees. To help address a concern that timekeeping was taking time away from officers' inspection duties, CBP implemented a standard process for tracking time in early 2007. The process includes estimating the amount of time officers conducting different functions (e.g., vessel or passenger inspections) spend on different activities, including customs, immigration, and agricultural quarantine inspections.

These challenges mean that statutory fee authorities that make fee collections available for obligation and expenditure for limited purposes may require more frequent review and updating for the authorized purposes to remain aligned with program needs.

REVIEWING USER FEES: PROVIDING INFORMATION ON COSTS AND PROGRAM ACTIVITIES AND FACILITATING STAKEHOLDER SUPPORT

By providing program information to agencies, stakeholders, and Congress, reviews can improve transparency, help ensure that fees remain aligned with program costs and activities, increase awareness of the costs of the federal program, and therefore increase incentives to reduce costs where possible (see figure 6). Reviews can also provide an opportunity to solicit stakeholder input on the fee and the programs it supports.

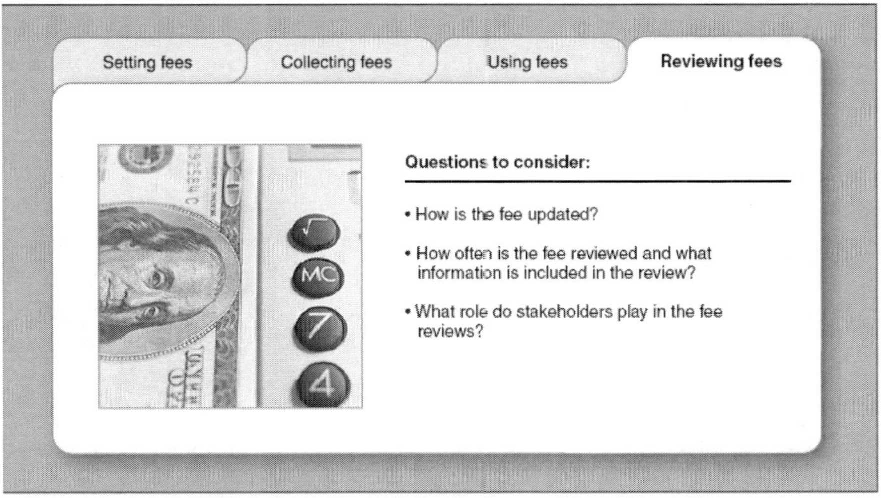

Sources: GAO (information); PhotoDisc (images).

Figure 6. Questions to Consider When Designing How User Fees Will Be Reviewed.

How Is the Fee Updated?

Fees that are not reviewed and adjusted regularly run the risk of undercharging or overcharging users, raising equity, efficiency, and revenue adequacy concerns. Fee rates may be adjusted by the agency (i.e., by regulation) or by Congress (i.e., by legislation) depending on the statute authorizing a fee.

When fees are adjusted by an agency through the regulatory process, fees may be updated more frequently than fees adjusted by legislation and this may improve the ability to keep fee collections aligned with changes in program costs. APHIS, for example, periodically updates the AQI fees through the regulatory process to ensure that collections are aligned with the costs of the program. However, in past reviews stakeholders have expressed distrust and concern about fee rates set by regulation because agencies that retain fee collections may have incentives to artificially inflate the costs of the user fee program. This risk may be reduced, and tools for Congressional and stakeholder oversight enhanced, if the agency clearly reports its methods for setting the fee, including an accounting of program costs and the assumptions it uses to project future program costs and fee collections.

On the other hand, when fees are specified and adjusted by legislation, Congress has more tools with which to play an active oversight role, but the fees may not be updated as frequently because of competing legislative priorities and other factors. For example, a fee for registering aircraft with FAA has been an insignificant amount since the 1960s.[68] Fees set by statute can, of course, be regularly adjusted. Such Congressional reviews and updates may be triggered in several ways, including a sunset provision. FDA prescription drug fees, for example, are authorized for 5 years at a time. A sunset provision, however, may not guarantee that a fee will be adjusted to reflect changes in program costs. Although the MPF includes a sunset provision, the maximum and minimum fees, which are set in legislation, have not been adjusted since 1995.

Congress may provide strict guidelines within which an agency may set fees through a regulatory process that may depend on further Congressional action. For example, the 2007 prescription drug user fee authorizing legislation set base fee revenue amounts for fiscal years 2008 through 2012. For each year after 2008, the law permits FDA to adjust the base fee revenue amounts to account for inflation and workload, and to set fees annually through the regulatory process so that total projected fee collections will approximate the revenue levels set in statute.

How Often Is the Fee Reviewed and What Information Is Included in the Review?

To ensure that Congress, stakeholders, and agencies have complete information about changing program costs and whether authorized activities align with program activities, agencies must substantively review and report on their fees on a regular basis. When a fee's authorizing statute does not specify review and reporting requirements, and for fees that derive their statutory authority from IOAA, the Chief Financial Officers (CFO) Act of 1990[69] and OMB Circular No. A-25 provide for biennial fee reviews that include recommendations about adjustments to the fees, as appropriate.[70]

The regulatory process is also used to provide information on fees to Congress and stakeholders and to solicit stakeholder input.[71] When an agency has authority to adjust a fee through the regulatory process, it should make substantive information about recent and projected program costs and fee collections available to the public through notices in the *Federal Register*. For example, in 2004 APHIS set the AQI fee rates for fiscal years 2005 through 2010. It published the new fee rates, along with descriptions of the costs of the program, projected program costs and fee collections, and the assumptions it used to make those projections, in the *Federal Register*.[72] Similarly, USCIS notified the public of proposed fee adjustments in the *Federal Register*. The notice provided information on the program's workload and the agency's methodology for determining program costs, including a list of program activities, how it accounts for the cost of providing services to users exempt from the fees, and its assumptions about inflation. For fees set in regulation, agencies must solicit stakeholder input by requesting comments in the *Federal Register*.[73] This provides an opportunity for stakeholders to comment on proposed regulatory changes—via written communication, not face-to-face conversations. As the passenger facility charge[74] user fee was implemented, for example, stakeholders provided comments regarding the fee, many of which ultimately were addressed in the final design of the fee. Nevertheless, we previously reported that nonfederal stakeholders have said that relying solely on notice and comment through the *Federal Register* is insufficient for obtaining stakeholder input.[75] In the past, APHIS solicited stakeholder comments as it adjusted the AQI fee, but it updated the fee using an interim final rule that took effect prior to the end of the comment period. Although an interim final rule does not preclude an agency from making changes to the final rule, stakeholders said that APHIS did not take their comments on the AQI fees into account because comments were not solicited before the change was implemented and because no changes to the fee were made during final rule making. Based on guidance from OMB, APHIS is no longer updating its fees using interim final rules.

Whatever the means for disseminating information about the fee, if the review is not comprehensive, it may not provide sufficient information to assess whether a fee needs to be changed. For example, we recently reported that the information on the MPF in CBP's biennial fee review was insufficient to either project fee collections or to provide assurance that the amount of the fee was aligned with program costs. This was the case because the review lacked projections of future MPF collections, the effects of exemptions, and changes in import demographics. We noted that without this information, CBP is not able to either determine if the amount, structure, or authorized uses of the fee should be changed or comment on the need for any changes to the fee statute. CBP's review noted that a detailed analysis of the current and estimated future effects of MPF exemptions, changes in import demographics, and a reliable cost estimate for processing merchandise are needed.[76]

What Role Do Stakeholders Play in the Fee Reviews?

Transparent processes for reviewing and updating fees help assure payers and other stakeholders that fees are set fairly and accurately and are spent on the programs and activities Congress intended. Also, because user fees represent a charge for a service or benefit received from a specific government program, payers may expect a tight link between payments and the cost of providing services and have expectations about the quality of the related service. Effectively communicating with stakeholders involves sharing relevant analysis and information as well as providing opportunities for stakeholder input. In past user fee reviews, we have reported that agencies that do not communicate with stakeholders miss opportunities for meaningful feedback that could affect the outcome of changes in fees and program implementation. Providing for stakeholder input may affect their support for and acceptance of the fee, and may contribute to improved understanding about how the fees work and what activities they may fund. Payers may also expect to participate in decisions about the provision of the service, including its form or quality. For example, in prior work on a proposed user fee for FAA services, we found that some stakeholders stated that if user fees are adopted, users should have more input into FAA's operations, citing the "user pays, user says" concept.[77] Soliciting stakeholder input is particularly important because government is often a monopoly supplier—that is, alternatives are limited so some fees are not fully voluntary—users cannot "vote with their dollars" as freely as they can in a competitive private market.

Agencies can accommodate payers' and stakeholders' input in various ways. The authorizing legislation of some but not all fees stipulates that the agency solicit stakeholder input in certain forms, including an advisory committee.[78] The immigration inspection fees statute, for example, directed the Attorney General to establish an advisory committee, whose membership consists of entities subject to the fees, to advise the agency on the performance of the inspectional services and the level of fees.[79] As we recently reported, the legislation that authorized the HMF did not establish an HMF advisory committee, although it did establish an advisory committee for a similar user-funded program for new work construction and rehabilitation on inland waterways.[80] PDUFA requires FDA to work with stakeholders, including representatives from consumer, patient, and health provider groups and the pharmaceutical and biotechnology industries, to develop performance goals for the FDA prescription drug review program.[81]

It is important, however, that actions are taken to ensure that fee programs do not become solely beholden to stakeholder interests. Where Congress and fee payers agree on priorities, there may be no conflict between oversight and accountability to Congress on the one hand and accountability to fee payers on the other. Where Congressional and fee payer priorities differ, however, the agency may be under greater pressure to satisfy the demands of fee payers, particularly when a fee is voluntary.[82] For example, although the FDA performance goals may be consistent with PDUFA's goal to improve FDA application processing times for new prescription drugs, a Congressional Research Service report on the fees cited some critics as saying that giving the pharmaceutical industry a role in setting program performance goals creates conflicts of interest and gives the industry too much influence over FDA actions.[83] We previously identified several promising practices for forming and managing federal advisory committees that could better ensure that committees are, and are perceived as being, independent and balanced. These practices include (1) obtaining nominations for committees from the public, (2) using clearly defined processes to obtain and review pertinent information on potential members regarding potential conflicts of interest and points of view, and (3) prescreening prospective members using a structured interview.[84]

Concluding Observations

The normative principles outlined in this guide are meant to present a framework for considering user fee design. Any user fee design embodies trade-offs among equity, efficiency, revenue adequacy, and administrative burden. Focusing only on the pros and cons of any single design element could make it difficult to achieve consensus on a fee's design. Instead, policymakers will ultimately need to balance the relative importance they place on each of these criteria and focus on the overall fee design.

There are always exceptions to any rule, however; as such, there will undoubtedly be cases in which policy considerations outweigh normative design principles. Nevertheless, the criteria, questions, and illustrative examples presented in this guide present real issues that policymakers must face when designing or redesigning user fees. See appendix I for a summary of key questions to consider.

Agency Comments

We provided a draft of this guide to the Director of the Office of Management and Budget and the Secretaries of Homeland Security, Defense, and Agriculture for review. We received technical comments from each agency, which we incorporated as appropriate.

Susan J. Irving
Director for Federal Budget Analysis
Strategic Issues

Appendix I: Key Questions

(We note that some of these questions may overlap.)

Section I: Setting User Fees

1. To what extent does the program benefit the general public and identifiable users?

a. Does use of the program by certain users, or for certain types of uses, provide a public benefit, for example, by advancing a public policy goal?
b. What is the users' ability to pay?
c. To the extent that the fees are used to replace funding by general revenues, what is the impact on the distribution of the burden of financing the program?
d. What would be the impact of a fee on users' competitiveness with others that would not be subject to the fee?
e. Is a similar service provided by the private sector? If so:
    - Will private producers be subject to unfair competition if the fee is not set to recover the full costs of the service?
    - Should their charges be a reference point in setting fees?
f. For programs that have not been paid for by fees in the past, has the value of the program been capitalized into private assets? If so:
    - Could transitional measures be used to address these concerns?

2. How will the fee be linked to the cost?
    a. Does the agency have timely and reliable cost data to link the fee to program costs?
    b. Will the fee recover full or partial costs?
    c. Will the fee structure include exemptions or reduced fees?
    d. Will the fee be set as a percentage rate or as a fixed dollar amount?
    e. If the fee varies, will fee minimum amount, maximum amount, or both be set?
    f. Will the fee structure be user-specific or systemwide?
        - Is the amount of the fee small or large relative to other costs that the user faces?
        - Are there numerous different groups of users?
        - Is the cost variation among the different groups of users large or small?
    g. Does the program have high fixed costs?
        - Is a two-part fee structure, with a flat rate plus a fee based on usage, appropriate?
3. How will the fee be structured to cover the intended share of program costs over time?

   a. Are fee collections projected to change over time in relation to the cost of the program due, for example, to inflation?
   b. To what degree will short-term fluctuations in economic activity and other factors affect the level of fee collections?
   c. Will the fee design include a maintenance of effort requirement?

Section II: Collecting User Fees

1. What mechanisms are available to ensure payment and compliance with requirements while minimizing administrative costs?
   a. To what extent do payment and compliance mechanisms impose administrative costs on the agency, the payers, or both?
   b. Do rewards and penalties for compliance correspond to performance?
2. Is there an agency or other entity that already collects or audits fees from the users?
   a. How will compatible policies and procedures and regular communication be established?
   b. How does coordination affect the administrative costs of fee collection for the agency and payers?
   c. Will collection by another entity affect compliance with fees?

Section III: Using User Fees

1. What degree of access will the agency have to collected fees?
   a. Will the fees directly support the related program or agency or be deposited to the general fund of the U.S. Treasury?
   b. Will agency access to fees be subject to Congressional appropriation?
   c. Will the budget execution of fee collections be through reimbursement, or will the agency receive fee collections directly?
   d. Will the amount of spending be tied to the amount of collections?
   e. Will the fee be categorized as mandatory or discretionary?
2. How broadly or narrowly will the activities for which fee collections can be used be defined?

Section IV: Reviewing User Fees

1. Will the fee be updated through legislation or by agency regulation?
2. How frequently will fees be reviewed and updated?
    a. Will legislation include a sunset provision to trigger fee updates?
    b. Will legislation direct the agency to submit regular fee reviews to Congress, different from the biennial fee review required by the Chief Financial Officers Act of 1990?
3. What mechanisms will be used to gather stakeholder input?
    a. Will the agency establish an advisory committee?
    b. Will proposed changes to the fees be published for comment in the *Federal Register*?
    c. What safeguards will be used to prevent the agency from becoming beholden to fee payers/stakeholders?

End Notes

[1] These are data on "user charges," which OMB defines as fees, charges, and assessments levied on individuals or organizations directly benefiting from, or subject to regulation by, a federal program or activity.

[2] See GAO, *Understanding the Tax Reform Debate: Background, Criteria & Questions*, GAO-05-1009SP (Washington, D.C.: September 2005).

[3] The price index values we used are averages of quarterly indexes from the Department of Commerce, Bureau of Economic Analysis' National Income and Product Accounts, table 1.1.4, last revised January 30, 2008.

[4] The Congressional Budget Office has defined user charges as fees or taxes that are based on benefits individuals or firms receive from the federal government or that in some way compensate for costs they might impose on society or its resources. See Congressional Budget Office, *The Growth of Federal User Charges* (Washington, D.C.: August 1993). For budget purposes, we define user fees as fees assessed on users for goods or services provided by the federal government. See GAO, *A Glossary of Terms Used in the Federal Budget Process,* GAO-05-734SP (Washington, D.C.: September 2005).

[5] See GAO, *Aviation Finance: Observations on the Current FAA Funding Structure's Support for Aviation Activities, Issues Affecting Future Costs, and Proposed Funding Changes*, GAO-07-1163T (Washington, D.C.: Aug. 1, 2007).

[6] *National Cable Television Ass'n v. United States,* 415 U.S. 336, 341-42 (1974).

[7] *United States v. La Franca,* 282 U.S. 568, 572 (1931).

[8] IOAA is codified at 31 U.S.C. § 9701.

[9] See http://www.whitehouse.gov/omb/circulars/a025/a025.html.

[10] OMB Circular No. A-25 does not apply to the activities of the legislative and judicial branches of government or to mixed ownership government corporations as defined by 31 U.S.C. § 9701.

[11] For more information, see GAO, *Principles of Federal Appropriations Law,* vol. 4, 2nd ed., GAO-01-179SP (Washington, D.C.: March 2001).

[12] Programs that primarily benefit the general public are generally nonexcludable, that is, there is no practical way of preventing someone from benefiting from the program, and nonrival, that is, once the program is in operation, there is no additional cost of providing it to more people.

[13] A drug sponsor is the person or entity who assumes responsibility for the marketing of a new drug, including responsibility for complying with applicable provisions of laws, such as the Federal Food, Drug, and Cosmetic Act and related regulations. The sponsor is usually an individual, partnership, corporation, government agency, manufacturer, or scientific institution.

[14] See GAO, *Tax Policy: Effects of the Alcohol Fuels Tax Incentives*, GAO/GGD-97-41 (Washington, D.C.: Mar. 6, 1997).

[15] In prior work on tax systems, we found that transparent tax systems enable payers to know their own tax burden and the tax burden of others, irrespective of who legally must pay the tax (see GAO).

[16] See GAO, *Congressional Attention Is Warranted When User Charges Or Other Policy Changes Cause Capital Losses*, GAO/PAD-83-10 (Washington, D.C.: Oct. 13, 1982).

[17] See GAO, *Livestock Grazing: Federal Expenditures and Receipts Vary, Depending on the Agency and the Purpose of the Fee Charged*, GAO-05-869 (Washington, D.C.: Sept. 30, 2005), and *National Park Service: Opportunities Exist to Clarify and Strengthen Special Uses Permit Guidance on Setting Grazing Fees and Cost-Recovery*, GAO-06-355R (Washington, D.C.: Feb. 9, 2006).

[18] See GAO, *National Parks Air Tour Fees: Effective Verification and Enforcement Are Needed to Improve Compliance*, GAO-06-468 (Washington, D.C.: May 11, 2006).

[19] See GAO, *Surface Transportation: Preliminary Observations on Efforts to Restructure Current Program*, GAO-08-478T (Washington, D.C.: Feb. 6, 2008).

[20] This study examined the overall fee collections of 27 agencies from fiscal year 1991 through fiscal year 1996. See GAO, *Federal User Fees: Budgetary Treatment, Status, and Emerging Management Issues*, GAO/AIMD-98-11 (Washington, D.C.: Dec. 19, 1997).

[21] MOE requirements help ensure that program funding from existing sources remains at or near historic levels before funding from other sources may be received. For example, federal grant programs may use MOE requirements to ensure that grants to state or local governments are used to supplement, rather than supplant, state and local program funding.

[22] The specified amount is the amount appropriated for the program in fiscal year 1997, adjusted for inflation as defined in statute.

[23] See GAO, *Food and Drug Administration: Effect of User Fees on Drug Approval Times, Withdrawals, and Other Agency Activities*, GAO-02-958 (Washington, D.C.: Sept. 17, 2002).

[24] This does not apply when the government, not acting in its capacity as sovereign, is leasing or selling goods or resources (e.g., offshore oil leases) or is providing a service (e.g., leasing space in federally owned buildings). Under these business-type conditions, OMB Circular No. A-25 guidance directs agencies to base user fees on market prices. Market rates are intended to promote economic efficiency and allow the private sector to compete with the government without disadvantage. If user fees do not cover the full costs of a service that is also privately produced, those private producers may be placed at a competitive disadvantage. Although reliable program cost information is not needed to set a market-based fee, the agency would still need this information to effectively manage the program, as discussed in Statement of Federal Financial Accounting Standards No. 4, *Managerial Cost Accounting Concepts and Standards for the Federal Government* (July 31, 1995).

[25] For more information on accounting for program costs, see GAO, *Managerial Cost Accounting Practices: Implementation and Use Vary Widely across 10 Federal Agencies*, GAO-07-679 (Washington, D.C.: July 20, 2007); *Managerial Cost Accounting Practices: Leadership and Internal Controls Are Key to Successful Implementation*, GAO-05-1013R (Washington, D.C.: Sept. 2, 2005); and *Human Capital: DOD Needs Better Internal Controls and*

Visibility over Costs for Implementing Its National Security Personnel System, GAO-07-851 (Washington, D.C.: July 16, 2007).

[26] Imputed costs of an agency are costs of goods or services incurred on behalf of the agency that are paid by another federal entity, such as certain retirement benefits paid to retirees by the Office of Personnel Management.

[27] See, for example, Bonneville Power Administration, *2007 Annual Report* (Portland, Ore.: November 2007).

[28] See GAO, *Federal User Fees: Substantive Reviews Needed to Align Port-Related Fees with the Programs They Support*, GAO-08-321 (Washington, D.C.: Feb. 22, 2008).

[29] Agencies must use realistic inflationary indicators if they want to reasonably estimate future program costs and better align future collections with those costs. OMB Circular No. A-94, which provides guidance to agencies on benefit-cost analysis for federal programs, notes that future inflation is highly uncertain and recommends that when a general inflation assumption is needed, agencies use the rate of increase in the GDP deflator from the administration's economic assumptions for the period of the analysis.

[30] See GAO, *Federal User Fees: Key Aspects of International Air Passenger Inspection Fees Should Be Addressed Regardless of Whether Fees Are Consolidated*, GAO-07-1131 (Washington, D.C.: Sept. 24, 2007).

[31] Marginal cost is equal to the cost of providing an additional unit of the good or service.

[32] There will be some loss of economic efficiency in either case: user fees set above marginal cost and taxes—that is, general revenues—both result in some loss of economic efficiency. See GAO.

[33] For more information on pricing for federal services, see GAO, *The Congress Should Consider Exploring Opportunities To Expand And Improve The Application Of User Charges By Federal Agencies*, GAO/PAD-80-25 (Washington, D.C.: Mar. 28, 1980).

[34] According to Statement of Federal Financial Accounting Standards No. 4, reliable information on the costs of federal programs and activities is crucial for effective management of government operations, which includes setting user fees.

[35] See GAO.

[36] See GAO.

[37] Unless fees are perfectly user specific, some users will pay a higher proportion of the costs they impose and some users will pay a lower proportion of their costs. In the case of a fee that is not user specific and recovers full program costs (i.e., does not use general revenue funding), some users will pay more than the costs they impose, essentially cross-subsidizing other users, who will pay less. See, for example, GAO, *Assigning Air Traffic Control Costs to Users: Elements of FAA's Methodology Are Generally Consistent with Standards but Certain Assumptions and Methods Need Additional Support*, GAO-08-76 (Washington, D.C.: Oct. 19, 2007).

[38] See GAO.

[39] See GAO.

[40] However, exemptions may only effectively address ability-to-pay concerns if exempted entities are aware of the exemption and have the capacity to make use of it. For example, a study by the Taxpayer Advocate Service found that nearly half of taxpayers below the poverty level, who should have been eligible for a waiver of the OIC fee, did not submit the form required to obtain a waiver. See Taxpayer Advocate Service, *National Taxpayer Advocate: 2007 Annual Report to Congress*, vol. 1 (Washington, D.C.: Dec. 31, 2007). The Internal Revenue Service revised the OIC application form and instructions in February 2007, and they now contain several references to the fee waiver.

[41] According to Corps officials, shipments into the port of Quonset/Davisville are not subject to the HMF because its harbor channel is not a federal channel and no federal funding is used for maintenance dredging of the channel.

[42] See GAO.

[43] OMB Circular No. A-25 guidance states that fees should be collected in advance of or at the point of service, unless appropriations and authority are provided in advance to allow reimbursable services. Regardless of the method of collection, the guidance requires agencies to ensure that the requirements of OMB Circular No. A-123 (Internal Control Systems) and appropriate audit standards are applied to fee collections.

[44] Lockbox services are provided by banks, which receive and process fee payments made by check or cash and send payment information to the agency.

[45] For fiscal year 2008, the fee for the prepaid AQI truck transponder is $105, 20 times the per arrival fee.

[46] See GAO.

[47] See GAO.

[48] With the creation of DHS in 2003, the customs, agricultural, and immigration inspections of international airline passengers were integrated into one program led by DHS's CBP.

[49] As outlined in OMB Circular No. A-25, the costs of administering and collecting the fee should be included when calculating the cost of the program and included in the fee rates when the fee is intended to recover full costs.

[50] See GAO, *Grants Management: Enhancing Performance Accountability Provisions Could Lead to Better Results*, GAO-06-1046 (Washington, D.C.: Sept. 29, 2006).

[51] Fees assessed by an agency under the authority of IOAA, rather than under a specific authorizing statute, must be deposited to the general fund of the U.S. Treasury and are not reserved for the agency or program that generated the fees, unless otherwise authorized by law.

[52] There are two types of offsets: offsetting collections and offsetting receipts. Offsetting collections are authorized by law to be credited to expenditure accounts (in effect, a negative expenditure) and are not subject to further Congressional appropriation before an agency may obligate the collections; an annual appropriation act may include limitations on the availability of obligation of these collections. Offsetting receipts are offset against gross outlays; are deposited in receipt accounts, which are generally dedicated to a specific purpose; and must be appropriated before they are available for obligation. However, most trust fund offsetting receipts are permanently appropriated and, therefore, can be used without subsequent annual appropriation legislation. A third type of collection, governmental receipts, is not offset against outlays and whether its use is subject to appropriation depends on the specific authorizing legislation for the collection. See GAOand GAO/AIMD-98-11.

[53] Because of the way the appropriation was structured, if the Corps were to obligate additional funds from the HMTF, it would have to reduce, by the same amount, obligations for other Corps programs. For example, in fiscal year 2006, Congress appropriated almost $2 billion for the Corps' operation and maintenance program. This $2 billion included amounts available for projects eligible for funding from the HMTF. If the Corps decided to increase spending on operation and maintenance of harbors and channels that is eligible for funding from the HMTF, the Corps would have to reduce funding for other operation and maintenance programs that are not eligible for funding from the HMTF, such as flood and storm damage reduction projects and aquatic ecosystems restoration.

[54] Trust fund surpluses add to the unified budget totals (increasing a surplus or reducing a deficit) and any trust fund deficits subtract from them. See GAO, *Federal Trust and Other Earmarked Funds: Answers to Frequently Asked Questions*, GAO-01-199SP (Washington, D.C.: January 2001).

[55] As noted in GAO, federal trust funds do not necessarily operate in the same way as trust funds in the private sector. Specifically, designation as a trust fund does not in and of itself impose a greater commitment on the federal government to carry out that specified activity over other government activities. However, the label trust fund may lead the public to expect a greater commitment, setting up unrealistic expectations. Stakeholders may expect that earmarked revenues—whether they are in a trust fund, special fund, or the general fund—

will be spent because the revenues are there, regardless of the need for the spending at the moment or the priority that would otherwise be given such spending.

[56] OMB Circular No. A-25 notes that it may be appropriate for an agency to seek multiyear or no-year spending authority if the program depends on user demand that is irregular or unpredictable.

[57] U.S. Department of Agriculture, Economic Research Service, *User-Fee Financing of USDA Meat and Poultry Inspection* (Washington, D.C.: March 1999).

[58] Mandatory spending refers to budget authority that is provided in laws other than appropriation acts and the outlays that result from such budget authority. Congress controls spending for these programs indirectly by defining eligibility and setting the benefit or payment rules, rather than directly through appropriation acts. Discretionary spending refers to outlays from budget authority that are provided in and controlled by appropriation acts.

[59] Although statutory PAYGO expired in 2002, both chambers of the 110th Congress imposed PAYGO through their rules.

[60] For example, recently enacted legislation extended trade adjustment assistance programs—programs for workers and farmers adversely affected by increased imports— for 3 months. The legislation provided offsets, including a 1-week extension of the expiration of customs inspections fees, to make the legislation comply with PAYGO rules under Congressional budget enforcement procedures. See Pub. L. No. 110-89, 121 Stat. 982 (Sept. 28, 2007).

[61] The budget resolution sets a cap, called a 302a allocation, on total appropriations for the Appropriations Committees. In turn, the Appropriations Committees provide caps, or 302b allocations, to their subcommittees. If a subcommittee were to exceed its 302b allocation, another subcommittee would have to allocate less. The section 302 allocations refer to relevant sections of the Congressional Budget and Impoundment Control Act of 1974.

[62] The Immigration User Fee Account is used to reimburse any expenses incurred in providing immigration inspection and pre-inspection services. Reimbursements are made on a quarterly basis. This has been a problem for CBP, since it has to use appropriations to cover initial costs and then later get reimbursed, raising concerns about revenue adequacy and administrative burden. Because CBP is reimbursed by USDA/APHIS on a bimonthly basis for its inspection activities, the APHIS fee raises similar concerns.

[63] In this instance, although Congress limited agency flexibility by limiting the use of fee collections, it did so in a way that did not closely link the fee to the program. Specifically, not all of the activities authorized to be funded by the custom fee are associated with conducting customs inspections, and not all customs inspection activities can be covered by user fee collections. In a recent user fee review, we learned that this created the misimpression among stakeholders that fees were being misused. See GAO.

[64] Congress authorized the pilot program, called the Recreational Fee Demonstration Program, in 1996. See GAO, *Recreation Fees: Management Improvements Can Help the Demonstration Program Enhance Visitor Services,* GAO-02-10 (Washington, D.C.: Nov. 26, 2001).

[65] Congress always maintains autonomy, as it can change authorized activities through legislation. Nonetheless, Congress has more flexibility as to how to use fee collections that are deposited to the general fund of the U.S. Treasury.

[66] To address these concerns and other issues, Congress passed the Federal Lands Recreation Enhancement Act (REA) in 2004. REA replaced the pilot program with new fee authority that increased agency flexibility for the expenditure of fee collections. Though, in general, REA requires that the collecting unit retain a minimum of 80 percent of fee collections, the agency may reduce the percentage allocation to as little as 60 percent if it determines that the collections at a given unit exceed its reasonable needs. See GAO, *Recreation Fees: Agencies Can Better Implement the Federal Lands Recreation Enhancement Act and Account for Fee Revenues*, GAO-06-1016 (Washington, D.C.: Sept. 22, 2006).

[67] See GAO. According to CBP, the agency has initiated a comprehensive review of its costs and activities related to merchandise processing, as well as MPF collections.

[68] The current House reauthorization bill, H.R. 2881, calls for substantial fee increases. See GAO.

[69] The CFO Act requires an agency's CFO to review, on a biennial basis, the fees, royalties, rents, and other charges for services and things of value and make recommendations on revising those charges to reflect costs incurred. 31 U.S.C. § 902(a)(8).

[70] OMB Circular No. A-25 provides that each agency will review user charges biennially. These reviews will include (1) assuring that existing charges are adjusted to reflect unanticipated changes in costs or market values and (2) a review of other programs within the agency to determine whether fees should be initiated for government services or goods for which it is not currently charging fees. It also states that if imposing such fees is prohibited or restricted by law, agencies will recommend legislative changes as appropriate. Further, the Circular instructs agencies to discuss the results of the user fee reviews and any resulting proposals in the CFO annual report required by the CFO Act. This reporting may be done in agency performance and accountability reports.

[71] Under the Administration Procedures Act, general notice for proposed rule making is published in the *Federal Register*. After such notice is published, an agency must provide an opportunity for interested parties to comment. 5 U.S.C. § 553 (b), (c).

[72] In addition, each summer APHIS publishes an annual reminder notice of upcoming user fee changes in the *Federal Register*.

[73] Executive Order 12866, *Regulatory Planning and Review*, requires agencies to provide the public with meaningful participation in the regulatory process, including an opportunity to comment on proposed regulations, which in most cases should include a comment period of not less than 60 days.

[74] Passenger facility charges are passenger fees that airlines collect and remit to airports. Airports use the fees to fund FAA-approved projects that enhance safety, security, or capacity; reduce noise; or increase air carrier competition.

[75] See GAO, *Reexamining Regulations: Opportunities Exist to Improve the Effectiveness and Transparency of Retrospective Reviews*, GAO-07-791 (Washington, D.C.: July 16, 2007).

[76] See GAO.

[77] See GAO, *Aviation Finance: Observations on Potential FAA Funding Options*, GAO-06-973 (Washington, D.C.: Sept. 29, 2006).

[78] Our prior work found that federal advisory committees play an important role in shaping public policy by providing advice on a wide array of issues. See GAO, *Federal Advisory Committees: Additional Guidance Could Help Agencies Better Ensure Independence and Balance*, GAO-04-328 (Washington, D.C.: Apr. 16, 2004). However, neither IOAA nor OMB Circular No. A-25 includes a requirement for agencies to establish an advisory committee or solicit stakeholder input related to their user fees.

[79] The Immigration and Naturalization Service User Fee Advisory Committee was first established in 1986. The Homeland Security Act of 2002 transferred the immigration inspection functions to the newly created CBP in DHS, and the committee was renamed the Airport and Seaport Inspections User Fee Advisory Committee.

[80] The purpose of this Inland Waterways Users Board is to make recommendations on program priorities and spending.

[81] See GAO.

[82] See GAO/AIMD-98-11.

[83] See Congressional Research Service, *The Prescription Drug User Fee Act (PDUFA): Background and Issues for PDUFA IV Reauthorization* (Washington, D.C.: Apr. 30, 2007).

[84] See GAO, *Federal Advisory Committee Act: Issues Related to the Independence and Balance of Advisory Committees*, GAO-08-611T (Washington, D.C.: Apr. 2, 2008).

In: Federal User Fees
Editor: Noah R. Myers

ISBN: 978-1-63484-868-8

Chapter 2

FEDERAL USER FEES: KEY CONSIDERATIONS FOR DESIGNING AND IMPLEMENTING REGULATORY FEES*

United States Government Accountability Office

WHY GAO DID THIS STUDY

Regulatory user fees are assessed on certain nonfederal entities subject to regulation in conjunction with regulatory activities. They represent a significant source of federal government revenue—some individual regulatory user fees exceed $1 billion in annual collections—and often support agencies' regulatory missions. Well-designed regulatory user fees can help fund regulatory programs while reducing taxpayer burden.

GAO built on its prior user fee work by assessing what additional design and implementation characteristics exist specifically for regulatory user fees in terms of how these fees are: (1) set, (2) collected, (3) used, and (4) reviewed. To do so, GAO reviewed relevant literature and analyzed 10 regulatory user fees within 6 agencies—Environmental Protection Agency, Food and Drug Administration, National Credit Union Administration (NCUA), Nuclear Regulatory Commission, Office of the Comptroller of the Currency, and Securities and Exchange Commission. GAO selected these agencies based on

* This is an edited, reformatted and augmented version of a United States Government Accountability Office publication, No. GAO-15-718, dated September 2015.

their high amounts of fee collections and rulemaking activity and diverse fee characteristics. GAO also examined stakeholder views on these selected fees and held a multi-agency panel discussion to ensure the broad applicability of the findings.

WHAT GAO RECOMMENDS

GAO is not making any recommendations in this report. NCUA provided written comments agreeing with GAO's findings. NCUA and three other agencies also provided technical comments, which were incorporated as appropriate.

WHAT GAO FOUND

GAO identified key elements of regulatory user fees for decision makers to consider as they design, implement, and evaluate these fees.

Source: GAO. | GAO-15-718.

Setting regulatory user fees: Congress determines in statute the degree of flexibility to make fee design and implementation decisions that will be retained or delegated to the agency. This has implications for whether agencies issue regulations to set fees, who will determine the level of regulatory activity, and how costs will be allocated among beneficiaries. In setting fees, agencies typically give special consideration to small businesses' ability to pay.

Collecting regulatory user fees: Regulatory user fees are not always collected at the time of a specific service or transaction. While some regulatory user fees are charged for specific services, many are collected from an entire industry at regular intervals as prescribed by statute or regulation. Collecting fees this way can create a stable revenue stream. Agencies may use different methods to ensure collection of fees because they cannot always withhold services until the fee is paid.

Using regulatory user fees: It is important to consider the availability of fee collections and unobligated balances. In some cases, agencies have the authority to use balances to mitigate revenue instability. In other cases, collected fees are only available to the agencies if Congress appropriates them.

Reviewing regulatory user fees: Regulatory user fee reviews provide important information for decision makers, such as identifying the effects of changes in a regulated industry. The appropriate time frames and methods for agency review will vary by individual circumstances. Regulatory programs produce both public benefits and services to fee payers, so it is important that fee review processes provide opportunities for input from stakeholders, including fee payers and the general public. Agencies can promote transparency by providing information on how fees are calculated and used to address the diverse needs of policymakers, stakeholders, and the general public. Decision makers can help mitigate the appearance that fee-payers have undue influence on regulatory outcomes through appropriate stakeholder involvement and dissemination of information.

ABBREVIATIONS

APHIS	Animal and Plant Health Inspection Service
CBO	Congressional Budget Office
CFO Act	Chief Financial Officers Act of 1990
EPA	Environmental Protection Agency
FCC	Federal Communications Commission
FDA	Food and Drug Administration
FINRA	Financial Industry Regulatory Authority
IOAA	Independent Offices Appropriation Act of 1952
MVECP	Motor Vehicle and Engine Compliance Program
NCUA	National Credit Union Administration
NRC	Nuclear Regulatory Commission
OCC	Office of the Comptroller of the Currency
OECD	Organisation for Economic Co-operation and Development
OMB	Office of Management and Budget

PDUFA	Prescription Drug User Fee Act of 1992
SEC	Securities and Exchange Commission
USPTO	U.S. Patent and Trademark Office

* * *

September 16, 2015

The Honorable James Lankford
Chairman
Subcommittee on Regulatory Affairs and Federal Management
Committee on Homeland Security and Governmental Affairs
United States Senate

The Honorable Jason Chaffetz
Chairman
Committee on Oversight and Government Reform
House of Representatives

Regulatory user fees provide a significant source of funding for government regulation, and some exceed $1 billion in annual collections. Thoughtful design is important to ensure that these fees can be used as intended to support agencies' regulatory missions and ensure that every funding source is carefully assessed. Building on our prior work on user fees, including *Federal User Fees: A Design Guide* (User Fee Design Guide) and *Federal User Fees: Fee Design Options and Implications for Managing Revenue Instability*, this report provides key questions for Congress, agency officials, and oversight bodies to consider when designing, implementing, and evaluating regulatory user fees (see appendix I).[1] Because the design of regulatory user fees varies widely and Congress provides agencies with different degrees of flexibility to manage them, some of the key questions identified in this report may be more applicable to certain agencies than others when considering individual regulatory user fees.

User fees are assessed to users for goods or services provided by the federal government. User fees generally apply to federal programs or activities that provide special benefits to identifiable recipients above or beyond what is normally available to the public. For the purposes of this report, "regulatory user fees" are defined as a subset of federal user fees that are charged to regulated entities in conjunction with regulatory activities.[2] Businesses and individuals pay regulatory user fees when they undertake certain activities subject to federal government regulation. These fees are often used to fund regulatory programs. For example, we consider the fees assessed by financial regulatory agencies and the Nuclear Regulatory Commission on their regulated industries to be regulatory user fees. We also consider application fees, such as fees charged by the Environmental Protection Agency to review applications for new pesticides, and inspection fees, such as fees charged by the Animal and Plant Health Inspection Service (APHIS) and U.S. Customs and Border Protection to people, goods, and means of conveyance entering the United States, to be regulatory user fees.

By contrast, businesses and individuals pay other types of user fees in exchange for the receipt of a discrete product or service where the government is not engaging in a regulatory activity. Examples of other user fees include entrance fees for national parks and fees paid for the purchase of certain government publications such as maps.[3]

We prepared this report under the Comptroller General's authority to conduct evaluations on his own initiative as part of our continuing efforts to assist Congress with establishing and updating user fees. Our objectives were to identify the design and implementation characteristics of regulatory user fees in terms of how these fees are: (1) set, (2) collected, (3) used, and (4) reviewed.

To do this work, we examined the characteristics of regulatory user fees through a literature review, case studies, and a multi-agency panel discussion. Our literature review included Office of Management and Budget (OMB) and agency budget documents; Inspectors General, Congressional Budget Office, and Organisation for Economic Cooperation and Development reports; and our related reports. We also used the literature review to define and identify regulatory user fees.

For our case studies, we selected 10 regulatory user fees within six agencies, as shown in table 1. We selected agencies and fees with high dollar amounts of collections, high amounts of rulemaking activity, and diverse fee characteristics. For each case study, we reviewed documents related to the fee and interviewed agency officials about their management of the fee, including the extent to which they found the User Fee Design Guide to be applicable to their regulatory user fees. We also examined stakeholder views on the 10 selected fees by reviewing public comments on proposed rules in the *Federal Register* and minutes of public meetings.

Table 1. Ten Regulatory User Fees Selected for Case Studies

Agencies	Descriptions of regulatory user fees
Environmental Protection Agency (EPA) EPA protects human health and the environment by developing and enforcing regulations based on environmental laws.	Motor vehicle and engine compliance program (MVECP) fee EPA collects MVECP fees to recover all reasonable costs associated with new vehicle and engine certification, compliance, and testing (42 U.S.C. § 7552).
	Pesticide registration service fee EPA collects pesticide registration service fees to cover the costs associated with the review of pesticide registration applications (7 U.S.C. § 136w-8).
Food and Drug Administration (FDA) of the Department of Health and Human Services FDA is responsible for protecting the public health by assuring the safety, efficacy, and security of human and veterinary drugs, biological products, medical devices, the nation's food supply, cosmetics, and products that emit radiation. FDA is also responsible for regulating tobacco products.	Prescription drug fee FDA's prescription drug fees pay the costs of the process for the review of human drug applications (21 U.S.C. § 379h).
	Tobacco fee FDA collects tobacco fees to pay the costs of regulating tobacco products (21 U.S.C. § 387s).
National Credit Union Administration (NCUA) NCUA charters federal credit unions and examines, supervises, and prescribes regulations for federally insured credit unions.	Operating fee NCUA assesses fees on federal credit unions for activities including the examination and supervision of federal credit unions (12 U.S.C. §1755).
Nuclear Regulatory Commission (NRC) NRC licenses and regulates the nation's civilian use of radioactive materials.	Part 170 fee for regulatory services NRC assesses Part 170 fees to cover its costs of providing regulatory services, including services to licensees or certificate holders (42 U.S.C. § 2214).

Agencies	Descriptions of regulatory user fees
	Part 171 annual fee NRC assesses annual fees to licensees or certificate holders designed to recover a percentage of its budget authority (42 U.S.C. § 2214).
Office of the Comptroller of the Currency (OCC) of the Department of the Treasury OCC charters, regulates, and supervises all national banks and federal savings associations, as well as federal branches and agencies of foreign banks.	Semiannual assessments OCC collects assessments from the financial institutions under its jurisdiction as the Comptroller determines is necessary or appropriate to carry out the responsibilities of OCC (12 U.S.C. § 16).
Securities and Exchange Commission (SEC) SEC oversees securities exchanges, securities brokers and dealers, investment advisors, and mutual funds.	Section 31 fee National securities exchanges and the Financial Industry Regulatory Authority (FINRA) pay Section 31 transaction fees to SEC, generally based on the sales of securities (15 U.S.C. § 78ee).
	Filing fees Companies pay fees to SEC for a variety of activities, such as registration or purchase of securities, mergers, consolidations, and proposed sales or other disposition of all assets of a company. These are collectively known as filing fees (15 U.S.C. § 77f; 15 U.S.C. §78m; 15 U.S.C. § 78n; 15 U.S.C. § 80a-24).

Source: GAO analysis of agency mission statements and other documents. | GAO-15-718

We invited 12 agencies, including the 6 named above, to respond to a questionnaire and participate in a structured panel discussion. Eleven agencies completed the questionnaire and 10 attended the panel.[4] In addition to the 6 agencies named above, the panel consisted of participants from APHIS, Federal Communications Commission, Federal Energy Regulatory Commission, and U.S. Patent and Trademark Office. These agencies were selected based on our prior reviews of regulatory user fees, as well as large amounts of regulatory user fee collections and diversity of fiscal and regulatory characteristics. In addition, we met with OMB staff to supplement information obtained from the case studies, questionnaire, and panel discussion. The results of the case studies, questionnaire, and panel discussion cannot be generalized to all regulatory user fees, but are designed to reflect the broad diversity of regulatory user fee characteristics. Detailed information on our scope and methodology is included in appendix II.

We conducted this performance audit from August 2014 through September 2015 in accordance with generally accepted government auditing standards. Those standards require that we plan and perform the audit to obtain sufficient, appropriate evidence to provide a reasonable basis for our findings and conclusions based on our audit objectives. We believe that the evidence obtained provides a reasonable basis for our findings and conclusions based on our audit objectives.

BACKGROUND

In our body of work on federal user fees we have reported on principles for designing federal user fees and evaluated several individual fees. Our 2008 User Fee Design Guide described principles for setting, collecting, using, and reviewing federal user fees.[5] That report examined fees using four criteria: efficiency, equity, revenue adequacy, and administrative burden. These criteria have often been used to assess user fees and other government collections such as taxes. We further reported on user fee design principles in *Federal User Fees: Fee Design Options and Implications for Managing Revenue Instability*.[6] That report describes six key fee design decisions intended to inform congressional design of fees that strike Congress's desired balance between agency flexibility and congressional control. We have also evaluated several individual user fees, including agricultural quarantine inspection user fees, patent fees, immigration fees, and air passenger inspection fees.[7]

As we reported in September 2013, user fee designs can vary widely and, in general, are governed by two authorities: an authority to charge fees and an authority to use fee collections.[8] Agencies derive their authority to charge fees either from the Independent Offices Appropriations Act of 1952 (IOAA) or from a specific statutory authority. IOAA gives agencies the authority to charge fees for a service or thing of value provided by the agency. Separate authority is needed for an agency to retain and obligate collected fees.[9] The terms of a specific statute permitting an agency to charge a fee would determine whether or not the agency can retain and obligate the collected fees.

However, Congress has frequently provided agencies with statutory authority both to collect fees and to use the collections. In these specific fee authorities, Congress determines the degree of flexibility to make fee design and implementation decisions that will be retained or delegated to the agency. Our September 2013 report found that in designing individual user fees, Congress can decide among options to retain its control or increase agency flexibility for various elements of the fee, including how rates are set, how collections can be used, and what reporting and oversight is required.

The legal and policy framework governing regulations is also relevant to the management of regulatory user fees. Specific statutory authority may grant an agency the authority to issue a regulation which creates rights and obligations, and addresses other substantive matters in ways that have the force and effect of law.[10] These regulations are generally codified in the Code of Federal Regulations.[11] Typically, regulations require a desired action or prohibit certain actions by regulated parties. The regulatory process is governed by statutes, executive orders, and agencies' policies and procedures that, for example, require agencies to evaluate the need for regulations, assess the potential effects of new regulations, and obtain public input (with certain exceptions) during the development of regulations. OMB is responsible for establishing government-wide financial management policies, such as OMB Circular No. A-25, *User Charges*. OMB is also responsible for ensuring that federal regulations issued by agencies follow executive order requirements and guidance.

SETTING REGULATORY USER FEES: THE AMOUNT SET CAN DETERMINE THE LEVEL OF REGULATORY ACTIVITY

Congress determines in statute the degree of flexibility to make fee design and implementation decisions that will be retained or delegated to the agency. This has implications for whether agencies issue regulations to set fees, who will determine the amount of regulatory activity, and how costs will be allocated among the various beneficiaries of regulatory programs, including small entities (see figure 1).

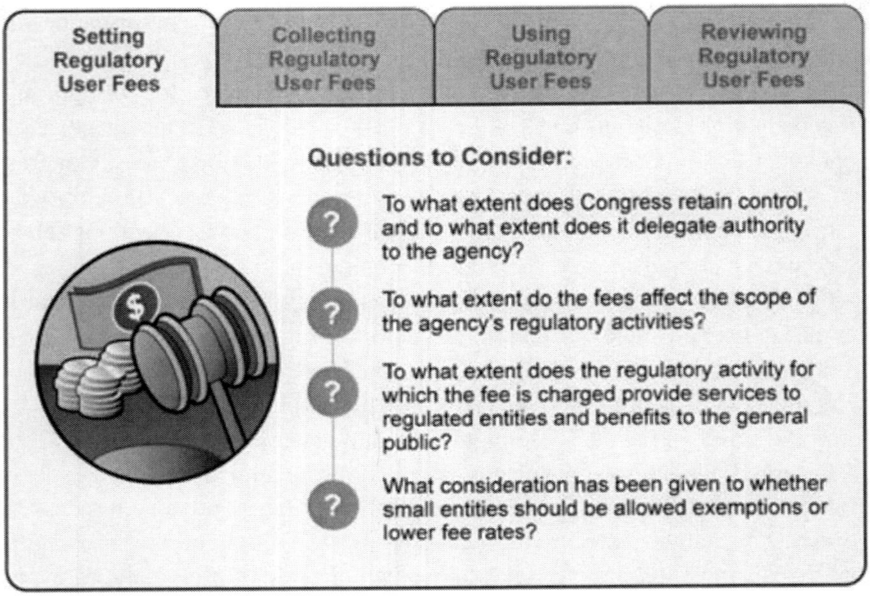

Source: GAO. | GAO-15-718.

Figure 1. Questions for Decision Makers to Consider When Setting Regulatory User Fees.

The Extent of Agency Discretion to Set Regulatory User Fees Has Implications for Rulemaking

As our prior work found, the degree to which Congress delegates or retains the authority to set user fees has implications for fee program management, including agencies' use of the rulemaking process to set the fees.[12] When an agency has greater flexibility, the agency typically sets the fee by regulation; when Congress retains a greater degree of control, fees are typically set in statute and agencies would not need to use notice-and-comment rulemaking.[13] The 10 selected regulatory user fees included in this report exist at varying points along this spectrum.

Examples of How Congress Exercises Control over Regulatory User Fee Setting and Delegates Authority to Agencies

- Congress sets in legislation the amount of the Environmental Protection Agency (EPA) pesticide registration service fee paid by each user.
- Congress set by statute the total amount of tobacco user fees the Food and Drug Administration (FDA) is authorized to collect each year, and established a formula in the Tobacco Control Act for allocating the total amount among the tobacco product classes that FDA regulates.
- Congress directs the Securities and Exchange Commission (SEC) in legislation to collect fees that are designed to recover the costs of SEC's annual appropriation, and prescribes a methodology that SEC must use to determine how much each user pays.
- Congress directs the Nuclear Regulatory Commission (NRC) in legislation to recover approximately 90 percent of its annual appropriation through user fees, but the agency has the authority to allocate the charges among individual users.
- Congress provided the National Credit Union Administration (NCUA) and the Office of the Comptroller of the Currency (OCC) with broad statutory authority to charge fees to fund their operations. These agencies set the total amount to be collected each year and establish the fee rates paid by individual users.

Source: GAO analysis of applicable laws. | GAO-15-718

Regulatory user fees can be set by notice-and-comment rulemaking or other mechanisms. The six selected agencies typically use notice-and-comment rulemaking to set regulatory user fee rates or structures in cases where Congress has authorized them to determine who will pay what amount. For example, the Clean Air Act, as amended, authorizes EPA to establish fees to recover the costs of its Motor Vehicle and Engine Compliance (MVECP) program. EPA uses notice-and-comment rulemaking to set MVECP fees and make changes to the fee structure. Similarly, NRC issues annual rulemakings to set the fee rates for its Part 170 fee for regulatory services—which is charged for direct services to applicants and licensees—and its Part 171 annual fee—which covers other regulatory costs. NCUA uses notice-and-comment rulemaking to establish its fee structure and uses memoranda to annually update the fee rates. In contrast, the six selected agencies typically did not use notice-and-comment rulemaking in cases where they do not have discretion to set or change the fee rate, or where a formula for calculating the fee is set in statute. In these cases, agencies communicate new fee rates by posting information to their websites, directly contacting fee payers, or using notices in the *Federal Register*, among other mechanisms.[14] For example, within approximately 30 days of receiving its annual appropriation, SEC publishes a notice in the *Federal Register* to communicate the new Section 31 securities transaction fee rates.

Fee Setting Decisions Can Affect the Level of Regulatory Activity

In setting regulatory user fees, decision makers can be faced with a policy decision about the scope of the agency's regulatory activities and the amount of the fee to be charged. Depending on its decisions, Congress may choose to provide additional appropriations to the agency. When regulatory user fees provide funding for an agency or program, Congress's or an agency's fee-setting decisions can affect the frequency, amount, or timeliness of the agency's regulatory activity because the total amount of regulatory user fees can determine the level of service or regulation that the agency provides. In some cases, such as SEC's Section 31 fee, this policy decision is made entirely by Congress because the total amount of fees to be collected is set by the annual appropriations process. In other cases, such as NCUA's operating fee and OCC's semiannual assessments, the agencies have broad discretion to set the amount of fees and use them to fund their regulatory activities. For example, OCC has statutory authority to collect an assessment, fee, or other charge from financial institutions as the Comptroller determines is necessary.

The effects of fee-setting decisions depend on whether the program is fully or partially funded by user fees. Some programs' only source of budgetary resources is the fees they charge. In these cases, regulatory user fees are often charged to an entire industry to cover the full cost incurred by the agency to regulate that industry. For example, FDA's tobacco user fee is the sole source of funding for the agency's Center for Tobacco Products, and it is charged to manufacturers and importers of tobacco products that are subject to FDA regulation. In other cases, regulatory user fees can be set to cover the costs of an additional level of service above and beyond what is funded by the agency's annual appropriations. For example, both EPA's pesticide registration service fee and FDA's prescription drug fee may provide additional resources to supplement annual appropriations and enable faster review of new pesticide and prescription drug products.

Regulatory User Fees Balance Public Benefits with Services to Fee Payers

Some agency officials participating in our panel discussion said that their fee-funded regulatory programs benefit the general public—either directly or indirectly—such as by protecting public health or economic stability, but pointed out that fee payers often pass on the cost of regulation to their customers.[15] Panel participants also said that fee payers can receive direct services in exchange for paying regulatory user fees, such as a license or the review of an application. For example, motor vehicle and engine manufacturers pay EPA's MVECP user fee in exchange for EPA assessing whether engines meet emission standards and issuing certifications. The manufacturers receive an EPA certification that allows them to sell engines, while the public benefits from cleaner air.

In some cases payers receive the right to engage in a regulated activity or business. For example, the tobacco manufacturers and importers who pay FDA's tobacco user fee can engage in the regulated business. Most of these user fees, as our prior work found, are spent to promote public health, such as through public education, regulatory science, product review, and compliance and enforcement.[16]

The intended benefit of paying a fee can also be a stable financial environment and consumer confidence. For example, the financial institutions regulated by NCUA and OCC pay fees for the right to operate financial institutions, such as credit unions or banks, and they benefit from the economic stability and consumer confidence that is supported by regulation of our nation's financial system.

Small Entities Are Typically Given Special Consideration

In setting fees, agencies typically give special consideration to small entities—which consist of small businesses and other small organizations, such as small banks or certain small educational institutions that handle nuclear material regulated by NRC. This can be an equity consideration that takes into account small entities' ability to pay the regulatory user fee and compete with larger businesses and organizations. These considerations can include exemptions or lower fee amounts. Of the 10 fees we examined, only SEC's filing fees and Section 31 fees do not have special considerations for small entities. The process for setting these fees is established by statutory provisions that do not take into account the size of the payer. Also, Section 31 fees are paid by national securities exchanges and the Financial Industry Regulatory Authority (FINRA), none of which is considered to be a small entity under SEC rules.[17]

In some cases, agencies are required by statute to provide special consideration for small entities. For example, the Pesticide Registration Improvement Act of 2003, as amended, provides for fee waivers for small businesses and for exemptions from fees in certain circumstances based on factors such as number of employees and volume of revenue.[18] Further, in our prior work, we found that the Leahy-Smith America Invents Act required the U.S. Patent and Trademark Office to establish reduced fee rates for micro entities.[19] In addition, when agencies set their fees by rulemaking they are required by the Regulatory Flexibility Act to consider the impact of these proposed regulations on small entities.[20] For example, EPA regulations provide that an entity may be eligible for a reduced MVECP fee if the full fee for an application for certification for a model year exceeds 1 percent of the aggregate projected retail sales prices of all vehicles or engines covered by a certificate, which is intended to ease the burden on smaller manufacturers. Additionally, agencies can provide special considerations for small entities when they are not required to do so. For example, NCUA and OCC—which have broad authority to set their fees—take into account the amount of assets held by the financial institutions that they regulate when setting their fee amounts. As a result of this fee structure, smaller financial institutions with fewer assets pay a lower amount than larger ones.

COLLECTING REGULATORY USER FEES: TIMING COULD HAVE MANAGEMENT IMPLICATIONS

Regulatory user fees are not always collected at the time of a specific service or transaction. Rather, many are collected from an entire industry at regular intervals as prescribed by statute or regulation. There are management implications for the timing of fee collections, as well as whether a minimum amount of annual appropriations must be reached before the fee can be collected (see figure 2).

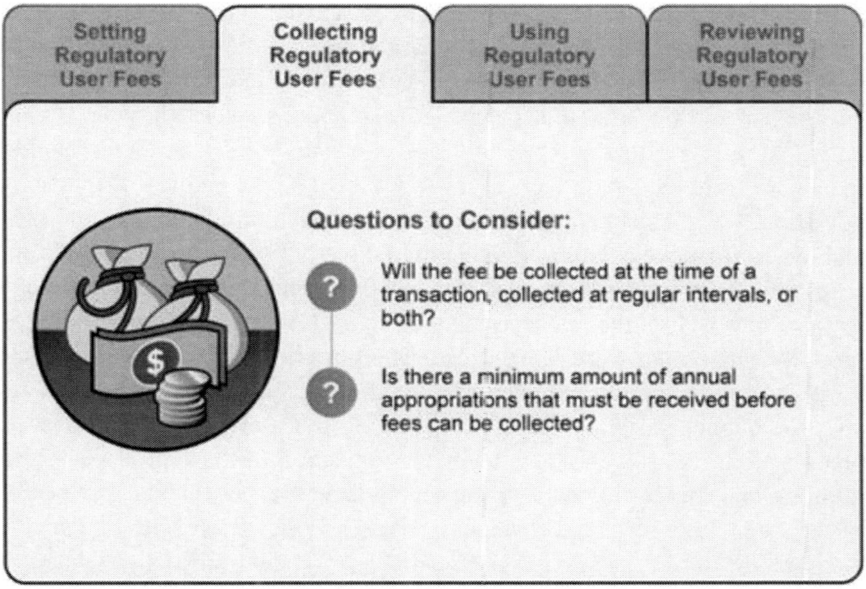

Source: GAO. | GAO-15-718.

Figure 2. Questions for Decision Makers to Consider When Collecting Regulatory User Fees.

Fees Collected at Regular Intervals Can Cover Broad Costs of Regulation, but May Require Different Internal Controls Than Transactional Fees

Six of our 10 selected regulatory fees are collected at regular intervals such as quarterly or annually.[21] Unlike transactional fees collected at the time of an individual transaction, these non-transactional fees include NCUA's operating fee, which is collected annually, as well as OCC's semiannual assessments and SEC's Section 31 fee, which are collected semiannually. Similarly, FDA's tobacco fee and NRC's Part 170 fee are billed quarterly, while NRC's part 171 fee is billed quarterly or annually.[22] FDA's prescription drug user fee includes both transactional charges for prescription drug applications and non-transactional fees, namely annual charges for establishments that manufacture prescription drugs and existing prescription drug products. In contrast to these non-transactional fees, our prior user fee work, including the User Fee Design Guide, focused on fees that are collected at the time of transactions for government goods and services.

Some non-transactional fees are charged to an entire industry at regular intervals to broadly cover the costs of regulating that industry. In these cases, the amount of the fee is not calculated based on services provided to the individual user or the number of transactions by the user. For example, financial institutions pay fees to NCUA and OCC to cover the cost of regulation.[23] The amounts collected are in part based on the amount of assets held by the financial institution, rather than directly tied to the amount of time or resources the government spends regulating them. Non-transactional fees can also cover costs the agency incurs in serving the broader public interest through regulation as well as other responsibilities not directly associated with services provided to the regulated parties. For example, FDA's tobacco fee pays for public education, such as educating consumers on the danger of tobacco products, as well as the agency's regulation of these products. Other non-transactional fees are collected at regular intervals but calculated based on specific regulatory services provided to the user. For example, NRC's Part 170 fee is charged for specific services provided to identifiable users such as licensing and inspection. NRC charges an hourly rate for these services and bills the users quarterly.

Fee collection procedures have implications for management. Internal control standards identify properly executing transactions—which can include fee collections—as a key control activity.[24] Accordingly, agencies need to have internal controls in place for all user fees to ensure that all fees due are collected and that each user pays the correct amount, among other things. An important element for designing these controls is having accurate and complete data for identifying and billing users. For example, FDA uses excise tax data when calculating the fee amount paid by each tobacco manufacturer and importer.

For fees that are collected at the time of specific transactions (rather than at regular intervals), agencies can ensure all fees are collected by withholding a service until they are paid. For example, EPA's MVECP fee is collected on a transactional basis and the agency uses two checks— one at the time an application is submitted and another before a certificate is issued—to make sure its MVECP fee has been paid. EPA will not issue a certificate if the fee has not been paid. By contrast, internal control mechanisms may take a different form for non-transactional fees, such as periodic inspections, as shown at left.

Methods selected agencies use to manage internal controls for their non-transactional fees

- SEC inspects national securities exchanges' and FINRA's controls and procedures related to Section 31 fees.
- After an assessment cycle, OCC checks a sample of the assessments to ensure financial institutions were billed the correct amount.

Source: SEC and OCC officials. | GAO-15-718.

One advantage of regular collections is that they can create a predictable revenue stream. According to FDA officials, the non-transactional elements of the prescription drug user fee—namely, annual fees for existing prescription drug products and establishments that manufacture prescription drugs—create a stable, predictable source of revenue, whereas revenue from the transactional application fees for new prescription drugs can be less predictable. We have previously concluded that the timing of fee collections can sometimes cause agencies to experience revenue instability. Specifically, collections that come in small increments on a rolling basis or late in the fiscal year may inhibit an agency's ability to identify overall patterns and fluctuations, or may create cash flow challenges.[25]

An additional consideration for managing regulatory user fees is whether fee collection is manual or automated. We have previously concluded that moving to electronic collections can reduce costs and mitigate risks, such as theft.[26] Moreover, two agencies—SEC and OCC—told us that automating fee collections reduces administrative burden. For example, SEC officials told us that improvements in automation would alleviate some of the administrative burdens related to filing fees. Specifically, many wire transfer payments lack adequate identifying information to post to the appropriate registrant's account and are therefore temporarily posted to an "unassigned" account. So SEC staff must research these payments and post them to the correct registrant account. According to officials, if SEC used additional payment options that required registrants to provide their account information prior to submitting monies to the SEC, it could eliminate payments going into the unassigned account. OCC officials also said automation has helped reduced the administrative burden of the agency's fee process, which was previously manual.

Some Agencies Must Receive a Minimum Amount of Appropriations before They Can Begin Fee Collections

The appropriations process can also have implications for the collection of regulatory user fees. Two of our selected fees have minimum appropriations thresholds that are established by statute. In other words, the agency must receive a certain amount of appropriations for the fiscal year before it can collect fees. For example, under provisions of the Pesticide Registration Improvement Act of 2003, as amended, pesticide registration service fees may not be assessed for a fiscal year unless Congress provides at least a set amount of annual appropriations for certain functions of the Office of Pesticide programs for that year.[27] Similarly, prescription drug user fees shall be refunded unless annual appropriations for salaries and expenses of FDA (excluding the amount of fees appropriated for that year) are equal to or greater than a specific amount.

USING REGULATORY USER FEES: VARIATIONS IN AVAILABILITY OF FEES AND UNOBLIGATED BALANCES

Considering key questions about using regulatory user fees can enable Congress and agencies to identify and manage issues related to revenue instability. As we have previously found, largely or wholly fee-funded programs do not necessarily see a proportional decline in costs when they experience a drop in collections. The authority to create or implement a tool to manage revenue instability may be retained by Congress or it may be delegated to the agency. Consideration of whether a user fee will fund a regulatory program includes determining the risk that fee revenue instability will affect the program and the appropriate strategies for managing that risk (see figure 3).

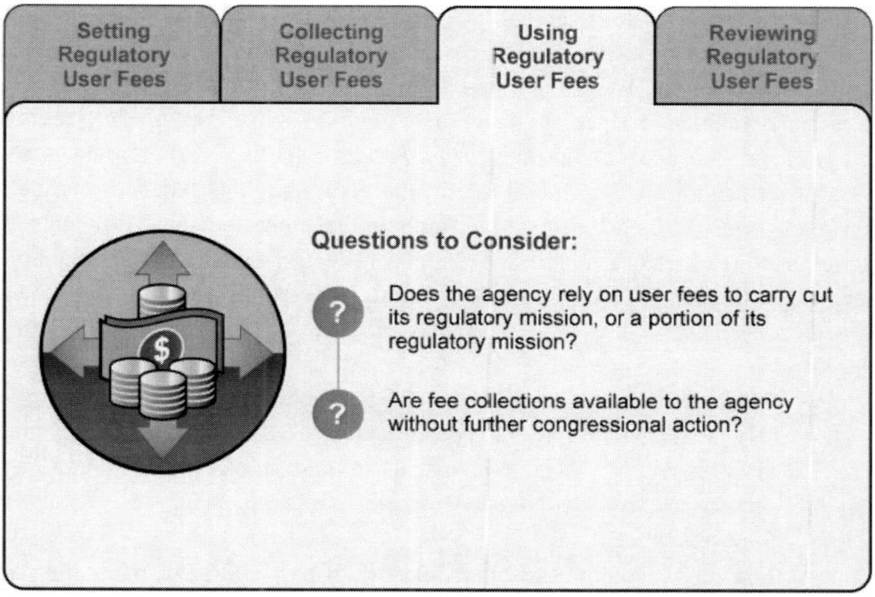

Source: GAO. | GAO-15-718.

Figure 3. Questions for Decision Makers to Consider When Using Regulatory User Fees.

Available Unobligated Balances Can Sometimes Be Used to Manage Revenue Instability

Some agencies have offsetting collection authority, which allows the agency to obligate against fee collections without additional congressional action.[28] These agencies may decide to maintain an unobligated balance as a strategy to manage revenue instability.[29] While the use of available unobligated balances to manage revenue instability is not unique to regulatory user fees, stability of fee revenue can be an important consideration when agencies rely on fees to carry out regulatory activities. As we have previously concluded, it is important that an agency develop a risk-based strategy when considering approaches to managing fee revenue instability.[30] This strategy would include identification and analysis of risks, as well as the effect on the agency's ability to provide goods and services.[31] Compliance with regulation is often a precursor to or requirement for engaging in certain businesses or activities. Sometimes fees are paid for faster and more predictable services and decisions from regulatory agencies. The agency must also execute its mission, such as FDA's mission to ensure the safety and effectiveness of prescription drugs. For example, each reauthorization of the Prescription Drug User Fee Act is accompanied by performance goals for FDA's prescription drug review program, such as goal time frames for FDA's review of new drug applications.

In our prior work, we found that available unobligated balances can help sustain operations for fee-funded programs in the event of a sharp downturn in collections or increase in costs.[32] The following agencies have available unobligated balances that they use to mitigate revenue instability for fee-funded programs:

- OCC maintains an available unobligated balance which, according to officials, it uses for unexpected expenses and to manage revenue instability. For example, OCC used these funds when it assumed certain supervisory responsibilities from the Office of Thrift Supervision in 2011.[33]
- The U.S. Patent and Trademark Office (USPTO) maintains an available unobligated balance to ensure its ability to maintain operations.[34] The agency began maintaining this unobligated balance in 2010 to smooth the impact of economic downturns on operations and to help address funding uncertainty.
- The Animal and Plant Health Inspection Service's (APHIS) largest fee comes from air passengers. Airlines collect the fee from passengers and remit it to the agency quarterly. APHIS maintains an unobligated balance to cover the time between the provision of services and fee remittance.[35]

Collected Fees Are Sometimes Unavailable to the Agency

Some collections are only available to the agencies if Congress appropriates them. Unavailable balances can accumulate in cases where the agency is authorized to collect more in fees than Congress appropriates. For example, at the end of fiscal year 2014, SEC had a $6.6 billion unavailable balance in its Salaries and Expenses account because, when SEC collects more in Section 31 fees than its annual appropriation, the excess collections are not available for obligation without additional congressional action. According to SEC officials, this large unavailable balance resulted from historical features of its Section 31 fee structure that are no longer in place. While in recent years

Section 31 securities transaction fee rates have been adjusted annually to equal the agency's appropriation, officials said in prior years the amount of fee collections was disconnected from the appropriations process. As a result, over the years, SEC collected more in Section 31 fees than Congress appropriated to the agency, which led to a growing unavailable balance, as shown in figure 4.

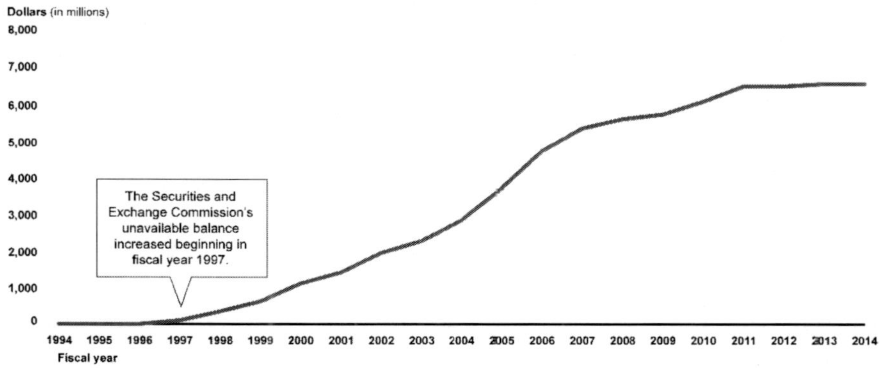

Source: GAO analysis of fiscal year 1996-2006 President's budgets. | GAO-15-718.

Figure 4. SEC Unavailable Balance, End of Year, Fiscal Years 1994-2014.

Similarly, the Environmental Protection Agency's (EPA) Motor Vehicle and Engine Compliance Program (MVECP) fee collections have not been made available to the agency. These fees are deposited into the Environmental Services Special Fund. However, according to officials, Congress has not appropriated money to EPA from this fund for MVECP purposes.[36] EPA has instead received annual appropriations which may be used for MVECP purposes. As a result, the unavailable balance of this fund has steadily increased. The unavailable balance totaled $370 million at the end of fiscal year 2014. In contrast, consistent with our findings from prior work, Customs and Border Protection's customs air passenger inspection fees are used to reimburse the agency's annual appropriations for a specific set of reimbursable expenses, such as overtime compensation and certain premium pay costs.[37] Similarly, NRC's user fees are used to offset approximately 90 percent of the agency's appropriation in a given fiscal year.

REVIEWING REGULATORY USER FEES: TIME FRAMES AND METHODS VARY, AND TRANSPARENCY AND STAKEHOLDER OUTREACH ARE CRITICAL FOR FEE REVIEWS

Regulatory user fee reviews provide decision makers with information important for deliberations about fee financing, such as identifying effects of changes in a regulated industry, but the appropriate time frames and methods will vary by individual circumstances. Given the mix of public benefits and services to users inherent in regulatory programs, it is important for fee structures and costs to be transparent. Agencies can promote transparency by providing appropriate information to address the diverse needs of policymakers and stakeholders, including fee payers and the general public. Through appropriate stakeholder involvement and dissemination of information, decision makers can help avoid the appearance of regulatory capture (that fee payers have undue influence on regulatory outcomes) (see figure 5).[38]

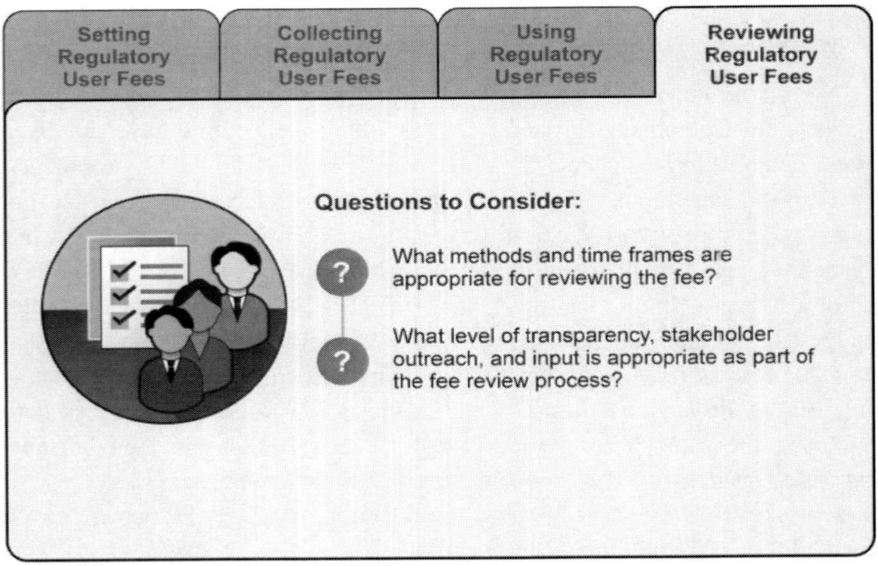

Source: GAO. | GAO-15-718.

Figure 5. Questions for Decision Makers to Consider for Reviewing Regulatory User Fees.

Fee Review Activities, Time Frames, and Uses Differ

Reviews provide decision makers with comprehensive information necessary to support robust deliberations about fee financing.[39] The regulatory agencies included in this report reviewed their fees regularly. Fee reviews take a variety of forms and the process and practice for reviewing fees—including activities, time frames, and uses—varied among the 10 fees we examined.[40] In contrast, some of our previous fee work found that agencies did not always conduct regular timely reviews of their user fees.[41] Further, we have previously concluded that fees that are not regularly reviewed run the risk of becoming misaligned with costs and consequently overcharging or undercharging users.[42]

Fee review activities can range from comprehensive reviews to ensure that fees are aligned with costs—as APHIS has done for its Agricultural Quarantine Inspection fee[43]—to simpler review activities such as checking to ensure that expected fee collections equal the appropriated amount. Agency officials described using a variety of fee review activities tailored to the specific fees. The scope of these activities can depend on whether the fee is cost-based and the amount of authority Congress has delegated to the agency. It is important for agencies to monitor internal controls to ensure they collect the correct amounts from all fee payers.[44] Statutes or regulatory processes typically determine how often specific regulatory fees should be reviewed. Through statutes, Congress may specify the frequency of fee reviews or give an agency discretionary authority to decide when to review its fees. Four of these agencies are subject to the Chief Financial Officers Act of 1990, which requires that they review their fees biennially and recommend fee adjustments as appropriate.[45] In addition, some regulatory user fees are reauthorized by Congress at regular intervals and undergo a more in-depth review during the reauthorization process.

Agency officials reported using Office of Management and Budget (OMB) Circular A-25, internal guidance, and guidance contained in statutes and regulations as criteria when reviewing their regulatory fees. OMB Circular A-25 is applied by agencies in their assessment of user charges under the Independent Offices Appropriation Act of 1952 and also provides guidance to agencies regarding their assessment of user charges under other statutes.[46] Some regulatory fees are charged by agencies that are not required to follow standard review requirements and criteria. For example, as a matter of practice, the independent regulatory agencies we interviewed told us they do not follow Circular A-25.[47] However, National Credit Union Administration

(NCUA) officials noted that NCUA will evaluate the concepts in OMB Circular A-25 when designing future operating fee assessments. Also, Congress includes specific criteria in some authorizing statutes, and three of the case-study agencies referred to our User Fee Design Guide for criteria.

All six case-study agencies conducted some type of fee review activity annually. Often these fee reviews were connected to the annual appropriations process, but the substance of the different fee reviews varied. Agencies characterized these reviews as ranging from budget management reviews to more complicated reviews that identified fee amounts and allocations across different payers and parts of the regulated industry, and are used to amend fee regulations. The following examples illustrate this range of review activities:

- Officials from FDA's Center for Tobacco Products, Office of the Comptroller of the Currency (OCC), and NCUA all identified internal processes to check whether expected fee collections are aligned with agency priorities, plans, and commitments.[48] For example, OCC officials stated that the agency's projected fees are compared to projected expenses, as part of the internal budget process, to ensure that fee levels are adequate to fund the agency.[49]
- NRC officials said their fee review process is integrated into its structured annual fee rule process and associated rulemaking. Most licensing fees are reviewed and recalculated annually using the current year budget and NRC's hourly rate for services provided to regulated parties. In addition, certain fees have been established as flat fees. NRC reviews these flat fees and small entity fees biennially rather than as part the annual fee rule process. However, NRC may adjust them annually if the hourly rate or time estimate for its services changes.
- SEC officials said they recalculate their fee rates annually as required by the statutory provisions authorizing the fees. Further, as required by law, SEC reviews its Section 31 fee rates midyear to determine whether an adjustment to the fee rates is necessary.[50]

Further, some fees that are reviewed annually undergo more detailed reviews during the reauthorization process. Some EPA and FDA user fees are reauthorized by Congress at regular intervals and undergo a more in-depth review during the reauthorization process. FDA's prescription drug user fee is reauthorized every 5 years. The reauthorization establishes the fee requirements and the process by which FDA establishes the annual fee rates and requires FDA to provide annual reports on its progress in meeting negotiated performance goals for the 5-year period. The reauthorization gives FDA, industry, and public stakeholders the opportunity to propose and discuss enhancements and adjustments for the next iteration of the program. Similarly, EPA has a 5- year cycle for reauthorizing its pesticide registration service fees, and fee reviews are conducted in conjunction with that reauthorization process. FDA and EPA officials noted that the information they provide as part of these processes supports deliberations by Congress and stakeholders about changes to the fee programs.

Reviews of regulatory user fees can be used as an important tool to identify and respond to changes in the regulated industry. We have generally highlighted the importance of retrospective regulatory reviews to, among other things, respond to changes in technology, market conditions, and the behaviors of regulated entities that cannot be predicted by prospective analysis before implementation of regulations.[51] Reviews of regulatory user fees can similarly capture such changes in the regulated industry that might affect the efficiency and equity of fees.[52] For example, according to EPA officials, their technical assistance in the review of pesticide registration service fees is useful in determining whether additional categories are appropriate. As a result of these fee reviews, the Pesticide Registration Improvement Act contains about twice as many pesticide user fee categories than when it was originally enacted in 2004. For example, over the last 3 reauthorization cycles for this program, the fee categories more than doubled.

Attention to Public Participation and Transparency Are Important Considerations during Fee Reviews

Decision makers identified different ways that they ensure appropriate transparency and opportunities for public participation when reviewing regulatory user fees. Transparency and public participation are especially important for regulatory user fees because these fees support a mix of benefits to the general public, not only to fee payers. In particular these principles are important for regulatory user fees because these fees are often a condition of engaging in a particular business. Further, there are diverse stakeholders, some of whom are not fee payers, who have varying interests in the implementation of these regulatory user fees and the programs they support.

For the purposes of this report, transparency entails disclosing information about the fee process with stakeholders so that regulated entities understand the amount they are paying and why, and other stakeholders understand how the fees contribute to a program's mission and expected public benefits. Public participation entails providing opportunities for all interested parties and stakeholders to provide input, not just regulated fee payers.

The forms of stakeholder engagement differed among agencies according to specific circumstances, such as the underlying statutory authorities and the amount of discretion the agency is given in setting and reviewing its fees.

- Stakeholder engagement requirements are clear when agencies issue regulations governing their fees. The federal rulemaking process provides standards for public notice, opportunities for comment, agencies' obligation to respond to significant comments, and the need to maintain a public rulemaking record. The public notices and rulemaking record aid public participation in the rulemaking process and provide access to the supporting facts and analyses for the agency's rulemaking decisions. Examples of fees set through notice-and-comment rulemaking include OCC's semiannual assessments, NRC's Part 170 and Part 171 fees, and EPA's Motor Vehicle and Engine Compliance Program fees.
- In some cases, Congress establishes specific procedures for periodic reauthorizations of the fee programs. For example, FDA's prescription drug fee reauthorization process includes regular meetings between the agency and industry, in addition to ongoing consultations between the agency and public stakeholder groups. FDA works with these stakeholders to develop a negotiated fee proposal, which it submits to Congress. For the pesticide registration service fee, EPA provides technical input to a coalition of stakeholders that helps develop the reauthorization statute.
- When an agency does not go through the rulemaking process to update fees and allocations, agency officials consider which alternative mechanisms are appropriate to communicate information about their fees and fee reviews, and to obtain input from stakeholders and the public. For some fees, agencies publish notices in the *Federal Register* that are not subject to stakeholder comment. This process is typically used when statutes specify a formula that the agency must

apply, and the agency has little discretion in updating the fee rates, such as with SEC's fees. OCC and NCUA officials said their agencies promote transparency by posting information on their websites when fees are updated. NCUA officials also noted using public board meetings to disclose information.

Our review of stakeholder comments from rulemakings and public meetings for these regulatory user fees showed both support for inclusive fee reviews and fee-setting processes, and concerns that agencies sometimes are not providing enough transparency. For example, FDA prescription drug fee stakeholders indicated support for the reauthorization process, which requires regular meetings between the agency and industry and public stakeholder groups, while some NRC stakeholders said that the agency could be more transparent about its fee-setting process by showing how it arrived at its revised fee rates. In addition, OMB staff pointed out the importance of agencies having sufficient understanding of how the timing of the delivery of fee services affects stakeholders. In general, stakeholders provided substantive comments about the equity of fees, administrative burden of fees, level of service, fee setting methods, and fee reviews.

Transparency and Public Participation Can Help to Mitigate the Appearance of Regulatory Capture

Some of the agencies told us that transparency and participation of all stakeholders, including public interest groups, can mitigate the risk of regulatory capture or the appearance of regulatory capture. According to FDA officials, the perception that there could be regulatory capture is a concern with some of FDA's regulatory user fees. To address this issue, FDA's prescription drug fee, among other fees, is structured in a way that minimizes that risk. For example, the performance commitments that FDA negotiates with the regulated industry focus on the regulatory submission review process—what will happen and when—and not the outcomes of the review. In addition, EPA officials said that the agency created a docket for pesticide registration decisions, such as risk assessments and proposed registration decisions, and allows the public to comment on them.

Case study agencies also described other management strategies to minimize the appearance of regulatory capture. For example, these strategies include separating fee payments from the outcome of regulatory reviews both in terms of the processes and the staff involved, and considering the diverse viewpoints of industry and public interest stakeholders in the fee-setting process. Further, OCC officials said that the agency's contingency reserve allows it to maintain its independence from the banks by providing revenue stability if a bank were to move to a different regulator.[53]

AGENCY COMMENTS

We provided a draft of this report to the Secretaries of Agriculture, Commerce, Health and Human Services, and Homeland Security; the Administrator of EPA; the Managing Director of FCC; the Chairmen of FERC, NCUA, and NRC; the Director of Enterprise Governance of OCC; and the Chief Operating Officer of SEC for review and comment. We also provided a copy of the report to the Director, OMB for informational purposes. We received written responses from the Executive Director of the National Credit Union Administration and the Executive Director for Operations of the Nuclear Regulatory Commission. NCUA's response agreed with our findings and stated that the questions identified in this report will be helpful when the agency determines future annual operating fee assessments. NRC's letter stated that the agency had no comments. We also received technical comments from the Department of Health and Human Services, NCUA, OCC, and SEC, which we incorporated as appropriate. APHIS, CBP, EPA, FCC, FERC, and USPTO had no comments.

Michelle Sager
Director, Strategic Issues

APPENDIX I: KEY QUESTIONS FOR DESIGNING AND IMPLEMENTING REGULATORY USER FEES

These questions can help decision makers design, implement, and evaluate regulatory user fees. They are intended to supplement the fee design questions in *Federal User Fees: A Design Guide and Federal User Fees: Fee Design Options and Implications for Managing Revenue Instability*.[1] While the key questions in those reports remain relevant for all types of federal user fees, here we provide additional questions that are specific to regulatory user fees (that is, fees charged by federal agencies to regulated entities in conjunction with regulatory activities). These products should be used together when designing, implementing, and evaluating regulatory user fees. We note that some of these questions may overlap. Further, we recognize that there is no one-size-fits-all approach to managing regulatory user fees. Because fee designs vary widely, when considering an individual regulatory user fee some questions may be more applicable than others.

Section I: Setting Regulatory User Fees

1. To what extent does Congress retain control, and to what extent does it delegate authority to the agency?

a) Is the total amount to be collected set in statute or determined by the annual appropriations process?
b) Does the fee reimburse the agency's annual appropriations?
c) Does the statute specify the fee rate paid by each user, or a specific formula or methodology that the agency must use to determine the fee rate?
d) Does the agency use the rulemaking process to set the fee rate?
e) In cases where rulemaking is not used, how does the agency communicate new fee rates to users?

2. To what extent do the fees affect the scope of the agency's regulatory activities?

a) Do the fees provide funding for activities that support the agency's regulatory mission?
b) Are the fees the sole source of funding for the regulatory activities, or one of multiple sources of funding?
c) Does the amount of the fee affect the scope of the agency's activities to carry out its mission, such as the level, frequency, or amount of regulation?
d) What role does Congress play in setting the total amount of the fee and the rates paid by individual users, and to what extent has this authority been delegated to the agency?
e) What role does the appropriations process play, if any, in setting the total amount of the fee?

3. To what extent does the regulatory activity for which the fee is charged provide services to regulated entities and benefits to the general public?

a. Is the fee paid as a condition of engaging in a particular activity or business subject to federal government regulation?
b) Are fee payers provided with a regulatory service, such as a certificate or application review?
a. Is the fee intended to fund a higher level of regulatory service than is funded by annual appropriations, such as expedited reviews?
b. Do fee payers receive an indirect benefit from federal government regulation, such as increased consumer confidence or industry stability?
c. What public benefits are derived from the regulatory activity for which the fee is charged?

4. What consideration has been given to whether small entities should be allowed exemptions or lower fees?

a) Does the statute require exemptions or lower fee rates for small entities?
b) For fees set by rulemaking, how will the agency consider the effect of the fee regulation on small entities, as required by the Regulatory Flexibility Act?
c) Will the fee structure account for any other policy considerations for small entities?

Section II: Collecting Regulatory User Fees

1. Will the fee be collected at the time of a transaction, collected at regular intervals, or both?

a) What internal controls will be in place to ensure that all fees due are collected?
b) For fees collected at regular intervals, what additional record keeping, data collection, or modeling, if any, is needed to ensure that fees are collected correctly?
c) Can the agency withhold service when the fee is not paid?

d) To what extent can fee collections be automated to reduce administrative burden and mitigate risks such as theft?

2. Is there a minimum amount of annual appropriations that must be received before fees can be collected?

Section III: Using Regulatory User Fees

1. Does the agency rely on user fees to carry out its regulatory mission, or a portion of its regulatory mission?

a. If so, what is the risk that the program could face an unexpected decline in collections or an increase in costs?

2. Are fee collections available to the agency without further congressional action?

a. If so, has the agency considered whether it needs to maintain an unobligated balance?
b. Does the statute establish a reserve fund, or specify whether the agency should establish a reserve fund?
c. If the agency maintains an unobligated balance, does it have a target amount?

Section IV: Reviewing Regulatory User Fees

1. What methods and time frames are appropriate for reviewing the fee?

a. What guidance should be used when reviewing the fee? Specifically, are the provisions of OMB Circular A-25 appropriate, or is there a need for program-specific guidance?
b. For independent regulatory agencies that do not follow OMB Circular A-25, is there a need for policies or requirements to ensure regular and timely reviews of regulatory user fees?
c. How, and by whom, will the fee review be used?
d. Are the fee reviews designed to identify meaningful changes that might occur in the regulated industry?

2. What level of transparency, stakeholder outreach, and input is appropriate as part of the fee review process?

a) Are fee review results communicated in a way that addresses the needs of the full range of stakeholders, appropriately addressing both fee payers and other beneficiaries such as the general public?
b) If fee changes are not done through a rulemaking, what alternative methods or venues can be used to communicate results of fee reviews and solicit stakeholder input?
c) How, if at all, will stakeholders provide feedback on the timing of fee-funded services?
d) How will the agency avoid the possibility or appearance that fee payers could have undue influence over regulatory decisions or outcomes (i.e., regulatory capture)?

Appendix II: Objectives, Scope, and Methodology

Our objectives were to identify the design and implementation characteristics of regulatory user fees in terms of how these fees are: (1) set, (2) collected, (3) used, and (4) reviewed. In carrying out these objectives, we also assessed the extent to which agencies found the User Fee Design Guide to be applicable to their regulatory user fees. To address all of these objectives, we examined the characteristics of regulatory fees using a literature review, case studies, and a multi-agency panel discussion.

Defining and Identifying Regulatory User Fees

Because there is no one standard definition of a regulatory user fee, and no comprehensive list of federal user fees, we used a literature review to define and identify regulatory user fees. Our literature review included Office of Management and Budget (OMB) and agency budget documents; Inspectors General, Congressional Budget Office (CBO), and Organisation for Economic Co-operation and Development (OECD) reports; and our related reports. We identified relevant literature by searching web-based databases and resources, including CBO and Congressional Research Service databases, the *Federal Register*, and ProQuest. We also reviewed the President's budget request for fiscal years 2015 and 2016 and searched for information on agency websites.

We included in our review any literature that we identified on user fees charged by the federal government to regulated entities in conjunction with regulatory activity.

To develop a definition of regulatory user fees for the purposes of this report, we analyzed the use of this term by other sources, including OMB, CBO, OECD, and academic literature. Based on these sources and feedback from the agencies we spoke with in the course of our case studies and panel discussion, for the purposes of this report, we define regulatory user fees as a subset of federal user fees which are charged to nonfederal entities subject to federal government regulation, in conjunction with regulatory activities.

To develop a list of regulatory user fees that meet our definition, we used the President's fiscal year 2015 budget request, agencies' congressional budget justifications, agency performance documents, and the results of our literature review. To ensure that we identified as many regulatory user fees as possible, we also searched for agencies with certain fiscal characteristics and high levels of rulemaking activity and corroborated the results of that search by reviewing agency documents. We determined that computer-processed data were not expected to materially affect our findings, conclusions, or key questions, thus rendering a data reliability assessment unnecessary.

Case Study Selection

We selected case studies of 10 regulatory user fees within six agencies based on high dollar amounts of regulatory user fee collections, high amounts of rulemaking activity, and diverse fee characteristics, including:

- agencies that are subject to the Chief Financial Officers Act of 1990 (CFO Act) and agencies that are not;[1]
- independent regulatory agencies and executive agencies;[2]
- fees that are intended to recover the full cost of operating an agency or program, as well as fees that are intended to recover partial costs and fees that are not cost based; and
- fees that are collected at the time of a specific transaction between the user and the regulator, and fees that are collected at regular time intervals (such as annually or quarterly) and not at the time of a transaction.

The fiscal and regulatory characteristics of our selected case studies are shown in table 2.

Table 2. Characteristics of the Six Agencies and Ten Regulatory User Fees Selected for Case Studies

Agencies	CFO Act agency	Independent regulatory agency	Regulatory user fees	Cost recovery[a]	Collection basis
Environmental Protection Agency (EPA)	Yes	No	Motor vehicle and engine compliance program fee	Full cost recovery	Transactional
			Pesticide registration service fee	Partial cost recovery	Transactional
Food and Drug Administration (FDA)	Yes	No	Prescription drug fee	Partial cost recovery	Transactional and annual collections
			Tobacco fee	Full cost recovery	Quarterly
National Credit Union Administration	No	Yes	Operating fee	Full cost recovery	Annually
Nuclear Regulatory Commission	Yes	Yes	Part 170 fee	Partial cost recovery	Quarterly
			Part 171 fee	Partial cost recovery	Quarterly and annually
Office of the Comptroller of the Currency (OCC)	Yes[b]	Yes	Semiannual Assessments	Full cost recovery	Semi-annually
Securities and Exchange Commission (SEC)	No	Yes	Section 31 fee	Full cost recovery	Semi-annually
			Filing fees	Not cost-based	Transactional

Source: GAO analysis of agency documents, applicable laws, and the President's budget. | GAO-15-718

[a] We examined the share of costs borne by the agency that these fees are intended to recover per their authorizing statutes and agency budget documents. We did not assess whether these fees are recovering costs as intended.

[b] Because OCC is an independent bureau of the Department of the Treasury, which is a CFO Act agency, when classifying agencies for selection purposes we considered OCC to be a CFO Act agency.

For each case study, we reviewed documents related to the fee, such as rulemakings and congressional budget justifications, and interviewed agency officials about their management of the fee, including how regulatory user fees influence the agency's regulatory mission and how congressional control and oversight affect the fee.

We examined stakeholder views on the selected fees by reviewing public comments on proposed rules in the *Federal Register* and minutes of public meetings. Our analysis included the documented views of stakeholders from the regulated industry, trade associations, public interest groups, and individual members of the public. We reviewed public comments on rulemakings to the extent they were available, which we identified by searching regulations.gov. Public comments on rulemakings were available for 7 of our 10 selected fees. For each of these 7 fees, we reviewed comments on from one to four rulemakings depending on the extent of comments the agencies received, using the most recent rulemaking available. These rulemakings were issued from 2000 through 2014. For 2 additional selected fees—EPA's pesticide registration service fee and FDA's prescription drug fee—we reviewed minutes of public meetings because no rulemakings were available. Specifically, we reviewed the minutes of three public meetings for the pesticide registration fee, which took place in 2012 and 2013, and the minutes of one public meeting for the prescription drug fee, which took place in 2011. We did not examine stakeholder views for SEC's filing fees because documentation of stakeholder views was not available. SEC officials said the agency has not issued any rulemakings or held any public meetings for this fee. To analyze the stakeholder views for the other selected fees, one analyst reviewed each source to identify relevant themes—such as the effect of regulatory user fees on small entities and the transparency of fee-setting decisions—and categorize stakeholders' comments related to those themes. A second analyst then reviewed the documentation to verify categorization decisions. Then, both analysts met to resolve any discrepancies. Finally, we evaluated the categorized information to identify common issues. The results of our review of stakeholder comments are not generalizable to all stakeholders, but provide insights into the views of fee payers, public interest groups, and other interested parties.

Questionnaire and Panel Discussion

We invited 12 agencies, including the 6 named above, to respond to a structured questionnaire and participate in a panel discussion. Eleven agencies completed the questionnaire and 10 attended the panel. In addition to the 6 case study agencies named above, the panel included participants from the Animal and Plant Health Inspection Service, Federal Communications Commission, Federal Energy Regulatory Commission, and U.S. Patent and Trademark Office. U.S. Customs and Border Protection officials also completed the questionnaire but were unable to attend the panel due to a schedule conflict. We also invited the Centers for Medicare and Medicaid Services, but the agency declined to participate. These agencies were selected based on our prior reviews of regulatory user fees, as well as large amounts of regulatory user fee collections and diversity of fiscal and regulatory characteristics.

To help identify topics for discussion at our panel, we developed and distributed a questionnaire to obtain these agencies' views on how regulatory user fees are set, collected, used, and reviewed, including the extent to which agencies found the User Fee Design Guide to be applicable to their regulatory user fees. To minimize errors that might occur from respondents interpreting our questions differently from our intended purpose, we pretested the questionnaire by phone with EPA and SEC officials. During these pretests, we asked officials to review the questionnaire as we interviewed them to determine whether (1) the questions were clear and unambiguous, (2) the terms used were precise, (3) the questionnaire did not place an undue burden on the officials completing it, and (4) the questionnaire was objective and unbiased. We modified the questions based on feedback from the pretests, as appropriate. We distributed the questionnaire on February 25, 2015, and asked respondents to complete the questionnaire within an electronic form and return it as an e-mail attachment. We sent follow-up emails to agencies that had not yet responded on March 6, 2015. We received 11 responses by March 19, 2015. To account for agencies with multiple regulatory user fees, we instructed each agency to answer the questions for the one regulatory user fees—or group of similar fees—with the highest dollar amount of collections in fiscal year 2014. Respondents from the 11 agencies that completed the questionnaire included officials from agency budget offices and program offices.

In addition, we held a 3-hour panel discussion with the 10 agencies named above on March 27, 2015. We used the questionnaire, as well as the preliminary results of our audit work, to determine discussion topics for the panel discussion. To do this, we summarized and synthesized this information to identify common themes. Discussion topics included the differences between regulatory user fees and other user fees, promising practices and challenges for managing regulatory user fees, fee reviews, and managing stakeholder relationships. We used information from the panel discussion to validate the themes identified in our case studies and ensure that they are broadly applicable to a larger set of agencies. While the results of the case studies, questionnaire, and panel discussion are designed to reflect the broad diversity of regulatory user fee characteristics, they cannot be generalized to all regulatory user fees. Because the universe of regulatory user fees is not defined, as noted above, it was not possible for us to design a representative sample. Throughout this report, we use specific, selected examples to illustrate how regulatory user fees are set, collected, used, and reviewed. We also met with Office of Management and Budget staff to supplement information obtained from the case studies, questionnaire, and panel discussion.

We conducted this performance audit from August 2014 through September 2015 in accordance with generally accepted government auditing standards. Those standards require that we plan and perform the audit to obtain sufficient, appropriate evidence to provide a reasonable basis for our findings and conclusions based on our audit objectives. We believe that the evidence obtained provides a reasonable basis for our findings and conclusions based on our audit objectives.

End Notes

[1] See GAO, Federal User Fees: Fee Design Options and Implications for Managing Revenue Instability, GAO-13-820 (Washington, D.C.: Sept. 30, 2013) and Federal User Fees: A Design Guide, GAO-08-386SP (Washington, D.C.: May 29, 2008).

[2] There is no one standard definition of a regulatory user fee. We developed this definition for the purposes of our report based on our analysis of the use of the term "regulatory user fee" by other sources and feedback from agencies included in this report.

[3] It should be noted that these definitions are not absolute and user fees can fall along a spectrum where an individual fee may have some characteristics of regulatory user fees and some characteristics of other types of user fees.

[4] U.S. Customs and Border Protection officials completed the questionnaire but were unable to attend the panel due to a scheduling conflict. We also invited the Centers for Medicare & Medicaid Services, but the agency declined to participate.

[5] GAO-08-386SP.

[6] GAO-13-820.

[7] A list of our related products is included at the end of this report.

[8] GAO-13-820.

[9] An obligation is a definite commitment that creates a legal liability of the government for the payment of goods and services ordered or received, or a legal duty on the part of the United States that could mature into a legal liability by virtue of actions on the part of another party beyond the control of the United States.

[10] Agencies generally have authority to issue regulations to govern the internal affairs of the agency, as well as interpretive rules that express the agency's policy positions or views in a way that does not bind outside parties or the agency itself.

[11] The Code of Federal Regulations is the codification of documents of each agency of the government having general applicability and legal effect published in the Federal Register, and are relied upon by the agency as authority for, or are invoked or used by it in discharge of, its activities or functions.

[12] GAO-13-820.

[13] For purposes of this report, whether a user fee is considered regulatory depends on whether it is charged to regulated entities in conjunction with a federal agency's regulatory activities, rather than whether the fee rate is set by an agency through regulation. Further, rulemaking refers to agency processes for formulating, amending, or repealing rules. Notice-and-comment rulemaking, as spelled out in the Administrative Procedures Act, generally requires agencies to: (1) publish a notice of proposed rulemaking in the Federal Register, (2) allow interested persons an opportunity to comment on the rulemaking process through submission of "written data, views, or arguments," (3) incorporate into the final rule a concise general statement of its basis and purpose, and (4) publish the final rule not less than 30 days before it becomes effective. 5 U.S.C. §§ 551-570a.

[14] Notices in the Federal Register generally do not go through the notice-and-comment rulemaking process and do not amend the Code of Federal Regulations.

[15] Although policymakers have determined that regulation can be in the public interest, regulations can impose costs on firms in exchange for achieving certain benefits, and these costs can be passed on to consumers.

[16] See GAO, Tobacco Product Regulation: Most FDA Spending Funded Public Education, Regulatory Science, and Compliance and Enforcement Activities, GAO-14-561 (Washington, D.C.: June 20, 2014).

[17] Section 31 fees are based on the dollar volume of securities sold.

[18] Pub. L. No. 108-199, 118 Stat. 419 (Jan. 23, 2004). This statute was most recently reauthorized in 2012.

[19] Pub. L. No. 112-29,125 Stat. 284 (Sept. 16, 2011). Micro entities are defined as small entities that are not named as an inventor on more than four previously filed applications, and meet other requirements. See GAO, Patent and Trademark Office: New User Fee Design Presents Opportunities to Build on Transparency and Communication Success, GAO-12-514R (Washington, D.C.: Apr. 25, 2012).

[20] 5 U.S.C. §§ 601-612.

[21] For the purposes of this report, we refer to fees collected at regular intervals as "non-transactional fees."

[22] Entities owing $100,000 or more are billed quarterly, while others are billed annually.

[23] While NCUA's operating fee covers the cost of the agency's regulatory activities, the agency's insurance-related costs are paid by transferring funds from the National Credit Union Share Insurance Fund.

[24] See GAO, Standards for Internal Control in the Federal Government, GAO/AIMD-00- 21.3.1 (Washington, D.C.: November 1999).

[25] GAO-13-820.

[26] See GAO, Budget Issues: Electronic Processing of Non-IRS Collections Has Increased but Better Understanding of Cost Structure Is Needed, GAO-10-11 (Washington, D.C.: Nov. 20, 2009).

[27] Congress has at times authorized EPA to assess pesticide registration service fees for a given fiscal year notwithstanding the minimum appropriations provision. For example, Congress enacted such a provision in the Consolidated Appropriations Act, 2014.

[28] Congress may choose to structure fees as offsetting collections or offsetting receipts. Offsetting collections are collections authorized by law to be credited to appropriation or fund expenditure accounts. Laws authorizing offsetting collections make them available for obligation to meet the account's purpose without further legislative action. In contrast, offsetting receipts are collections that are offset against gross outlays but are not authorized to be credited to expenditure accounts. Unlike offsetting collections, offsetting receipts cannot be used without being appropriated.

[29] An available unobligated balance is budget authority that has not yet been obligated. For more information on balances in federal accounts, see GAO, Budget Issues: Key Questions to Consider When Evaluating Balances in Federal Accounts, GAO-13-798 (Washington, D.C.: Sept. 30, 2013). Agencies sometimes refer to an available unobligated balance as a "reserve fund."

[30] GAO-13-820.

[31] GAO-13-820. This work included regulatory user fees and other user fees. [32] GAO-13-820.

[33] The Dodd-Frank Wall Street Reform and Consumer Protection Act eliminated the Office of Thrift Supervision. Supervisory authority for federal savings associations was transferred to OCC. The transfer of these powers was completed on July 21, 2011.

[34] The available unobligated balance (also referred to as the "operating reserve") is a portion of USPTO's annual appropriation set aside by the agency. It appears on USPTO's financial statements and OMB's budget database as an unobligated balance. The operating reserve is separate and distinct from the Patent and Trademark Fee Reserve Fund, which is a separate account established by the America Invents Act that is available to USPTO to the extent appropriated by Congress.

[35] We previously recommended that the Secretary of Agriculture establish a target reserve for the agricultural quarantine inspection fee that is more closely aligned with program needs and risks. See GAO, Agricultural Quarantine Inspection Fees: Major Changes Needed to Align Fee Revenues with Program Costs, GAO-13-268 (Washington, D.C.: Mar. 1, 2013). The Department of Agriculture agreed with the recommendation and in April 2014 issued a proposed rule that would adjust its fee structure and establish a reserve equal to 90 days of operating costs. According to an APHIS official, as of June 2015, a draft final rule to amend the AQI fees was under review by the Office of Management and Budget.

[36] The Environmental Services Special Fund also contains other moneys, including Lead Accreditation and Certification fee collections.

[37] See GAO, Federal User Fees: Key Aspects of International Air Passenger Inspection Fees Should Be Addressed Regardless of Whether Fees Are Consolidated, GAO-07-1131 (Washington, D.C.: Sept. 24, 2007).

[38] Regulatory capture occurs when an agency becomes dominated by the industry it is charged with regulating and acts in ways that benefit the industry rather than the public interest.

[39] Among the general benefits of user fee reviews are that they: (1) help to ensure that Congress, stakeholders, and agencies have complete information about changing costs and whether a fee needs to be changed; (2) help agencies determine if they are prepared for any spikes or

surges in demand; (3) help agencies and fee payers avoid a sudden increase in fee rates due to misalignment between costs and collections; (4) provide opportunities for stakeholder input; and (5) promote understanding and acceptance of the fee.

[40] For the purposes of this report, we are including any of the processes by which agencies evaluate, verify, or update regulatory user fees in our discussion of fee reviews.

[41] For example, in 2011 we surveyed the 24 agencies covered by the Chief Financial Officers Act of 1990. These agencies reported reviewing about 46 percent of the 3,666 fees charged. See GAO, 2012 Annual Report: Opportunities to Reduce Duplication, Overlap and Fragmentation, Achieve Savings, and Enhance Revenue, GAO-12-342SP (Washington, D.C.: Feb. 28, 2012).

[42] A list of our related products is included at the end of this report.

[43] We previously reported that in 2010, APHIS hired a contractor to conduct a comprehensive fee review to determine the full cost of agricultural quarantine inspection services, identify potential changes to the fee structure, and recommend new fees. See GAO-13-268.

[44] GAO/AIMD-00-21.3.1.

[45] Chief Financial Officers Act of 1990, Pub. L. No. 101-576 (Nov. 15, 1990), codified at 31 U.S.C. § 902.

[46] Circular A-25 covers all federal activities that convey special benefits to recipients beyond those accruing to the general public. It does not apply to the activities of the legislative and judicial branches of government or to mixed-ownership government corporations, as defined in 31 U.S.C. § 9701. Further, OMB staff told us they believe Circular A-25 provides good management principles for setting and reviewing user fees that can be applied to independent entities.

[47] "Independent regulatory agencies" refer to the agencies identified as such in the Paperwork Reduction Act. 44 U.S.C. § 3502.

[48] NCUA's authorizing statute provides broad discretion to NCUA's Board to review and set its fees annually or according to any method that it deems appropriate.

[49] OCC's funding is not provided through annual appropriations and assessments, charges, or fees collected by OCC "shall not be construed to be Government funds or appropriated moneys" pursuant to 12 U.S.C. § 16.

[50] While SEC does not consider this process to be a fee review because the statute defines how the agency should update fees and it has little discretion, the process resembles a fee review because it is designed to ensure that the agency collects the correct amount.

[51] GAO, Reexamining Regulations: Agencies Often Made Regulatory Changes, but Could Strengthen Linkages to Performance Goals, GAO-14-268 (Washington, D.C.: Apr. 11, 2014).

[52] See also GAO, Federal Communications Commission: Regulatory Fee Process Needs to Be Updated, GAO-12-686 (Washington, D.C.: Aug. 10, 2012), in which we recommended, among other things, that the Federal Communications Commission (FCC) should perform an updated FTE analysis when assessing regulatory fees among industry sectors to address major changes in the telecommunications industry. According to FCC officials, FCC has taken steps to address these recommendations through notices of proposed rulemaking and regulatory fees reports and orders in 2013 and 2014. As of August 2015, we were in the process of evaluating FCC's efforts in this area.

[53] Banks decide where they are chartered. State chartered banks are supervised by the states and the Board of Governors of the Federal Reserve System or Federal Deposit Insurance Corporation.

End Note for Appendix I

[1] See GAO, Federal User Fees: Fee Design Options and Implications for Managing Revenue Instability, GAO-13-820 (Washington, D.C.: Sept. 30, 2013) and Federal User Fees: A Design Guide, GAO-08-386SP (Washington, D.C.: May 29, 2008).

End Notes for Appendix II

[1] 31 U.S.C. § 902(a)(8). This statute requires affected agencies to review fees on a biennial basis.

[2] For purposes of this report, “independent regulatory agencies” refers to those agencies designated as such in the Paperwork Reduction Act, 44 U.S.C. § 3502. They have historically been subject to less executive branch oversight than executive agencies.

In: Federal User Fees
Editor: Noah R. Myers
ISBN: 978-1-63484-868-8

Chapter 3

FEDERAL USER FEES: FEE DESIGN OPTIONS AND IMPLICATIONS FOR MANAGING REVENUE INSTABILITY*

United States Government Accountability Office

WHY GAO DID THIS STUDY

In 2012, the President's Budget reported nearly $300 billion collected in user fees from the public. Given the nation's fiscal condition it is critical that every funding source and spending decision be carefully considered and applied to its best use. GAO was asked to review oversight opportunities for fees. GAO examined (1) key Congressional design decisions and related implications for achieving the desired balance between agency flexibility and congressional control, (2) issues related to identifying and managing unobligated balances in selected fee-funded agencies, and (3) key questions to identify potential sources of fee revenue instability and to manage any consequences. To do so, GAO analyzed laws, agency documents and guidance, literature, and prior GAO work. In addition, GAO interviewed officials at three fully fee-funded agencies, which were selected to illustrate implications of key design options, unobligated fee balances, and approaches

* This is an edited, reformatted and augmented version of a United States Government Accountability Office publication, No. GAO-13-820, dated September 2013.

for managing revenue instability. GAO also validated certain findings with budget subject matter specialists.

WHAT GAO RECOMMENDS

GAO is not making any new recommendations in this report. GAO previously recommended that the Office of Management and Budget (OMB) review fee-funded programs and identify opportunities to improve their design and better align fee collections with program costs. OMB has not yet taken action on this recommendation. Two of the three selected fully fee-funded agencies provided technical comments which were incorporated as appropriate.

WHAT GAO FOUND

GAO identified six key fee design decisions related to how fees are set, used, and reviewed that, in the aggregate, enable Congress to design fees that strike the desired balance between agency flexibility and congressional control (see figure below). For example, narrowly limiting the activities for which fees may be used heightens congressional control over the funds; however, doing so can also reduce an agency's flexibility to reallocate resources as needs change and may increase administrative costs. Design decisions also have program management implications. For example, the frequency of fee reviews and adjustments affects the alignment between collections and costs. Failing to review fees regularly has sometimes resulted in large increases when fees are eventually updated, creating costly challenges. Understanding the implications of fee design is important to avoid such unintended consequences.

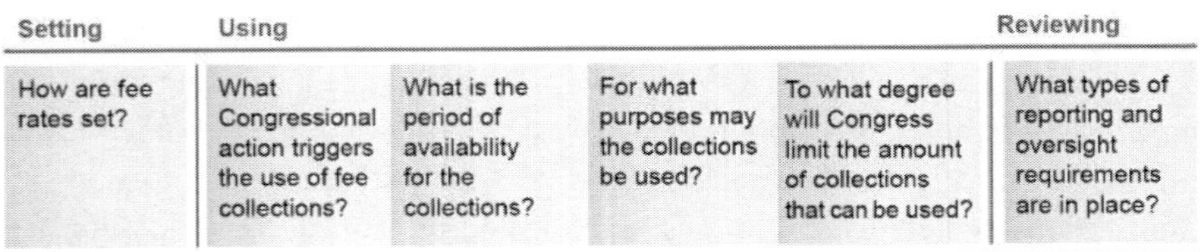

Source: GAO.

Congressional Fee Design Decisions Key to Determining Agency Flexibility and Congressional Control.

Identifying and understanding unobligated balances—the portion of obligational authority that has not yet been obligated—in fee-based accounts is challenging. There is no single list of all federal user fees, and in general, budget accounts are not labeled in a way that indicates whether an account contains fee collections. This makes it challenging to identify whether (or which) unobligated balances in an account are fee-related. Further, some fee designs include dedicated reserves that appear as unobligated balances. Despite these challenges, funding a program or agency through fees does not eliminate the need for careful monitoring and managing of unobligated balances.

Considering key questions about costs and collections can enable Congress and agencies to identify and manage potential fluctuations in fee collections–known as revenue instability–as well as potential consequences. Importantly, decision makers need to understand potential vulnerabilities in the context of a fee's design. Examples of such questions include: what is the risk that fee revenue instability will affect a program? What analysis is needed to understand factors such as cost drivers and elements that influence collections? Are there data limitations that could add uncertainty to collection estimates? Can the agency quickly respond to changing costs? What factors affect the timing and pattern of collections and spending? If revenue instability is a function of a fee's design, the most sustainable solutions are often found by realigning costs and collections. In other cases, maintaining a reserve can help address sudden or temporary fluctuations in collections and/or costs and can minimize the effect of revenue instability on operations.

ABBREVIATIONS

AIA	Leahy-Smith America Invents Act of 2011
APHIS	Animal and Plant Health Inspection Service
AQI	Agricultural Quarantine Inspection
CBP	Customs and Border Protection
CBO	Congressional Budget Office
CFO Act	Chief Financial Officers Act of 1990
COBRA	Consolidated Omnibus Reconciliation Act of 1985
FCC	Federal Communications Commission
IOAA	Independent Offices Appropriation Act of 1952
OMB	Office of Management and Budget
PEF	Public Enterprise Fund

Mint	United States Mint
USAC	Universal Service Administrative Company
USCIS	United States Citizenship and Immigration Service
USF	Universal Service Fund
USPTO	United States Patent and Trademark Office

* * *

September 30, 2013

The Honorable Paul Ryan
Chairman
Committee on the Budget
House of Representatives

Dear Mr. Chairman:

In 2012, the federal government collected nearly $300 billion in user fees from the public.[1] Given the nation's fiscal condition, it is critical that every funding source and spending decision be carefully considered and applied to its best use.[2] As funds become increasingly scarce and new policy priorities emerge, policymakers have demonstrated interest in user fees as a means of financing new and existing services. Well designed fees can fund programs or activities that benefit an identifiable population beyond what is normally provided to the public, while promoting economic efficiency and equity.

You asked us to provide information on the key appropriations frameworks used to design federal user fees and charges, on the unobligated balances in selected fee accounts—specifically, the portion of obligational authority that has not yet been obligated—and on some key questions Congress and agencies could consider when overseeing and managing fee revenue instability. Our objectives were (1) to identify the key Congressional design decisions and related implications for achieving the desired balance between agency flexibility and Congressional control, (2) to examine issues related to identifying and managing unobligated balances in selected fee-funded agencies, and (3) to identify key questions to identify potential sources of fee revenue instability and manage any consequences.

To identify the key Congressional design decisions for achieving the desired levels of agency flexibility and Congressional control, we reviewed our prior work, including *Federal User Fees: A Design Guide*,[3] and selected user fee statutory authorities and regulations and met with the Congressional Budget Office. We also reviewed relevant user fee policies contained in the Office of Management and Budget's (OMB) Circular A-25 and contained in the Chief Financial Officers Act of 1990 (CFO Act).[4]

To review unobligated balances derived from fees, we reviewed fiscal year 2007 through 2011 unobligated balance data from OMB's MAX database, agency congressional justifications, and agency financial documents. We also reviewed data from our 2011 survey of fee collections in agencies covered by the CFO Act and OMB Circular A-25 that we collected for our annual review of program duplication, overlap, and fragmentation.[5] In addition, we reviewed congressional budget justifications and financial reports from agencies not covered by the CFO Act. We reviewed the amount of fees collected and the statutory authorities governing collection and use of fees. Based on this, we selected three fully fee-funded agencies— the United States Mint (the Mint) in the Department of the Treasury, the United States Patent and Trademark Office (USPTO) in the Department of Commerce, and the Federal Communications Commission (FCC). Although the results from these three agencies may not be generalized to all fee-funded agencies, the selection of these agencies was appropriate to illustrate implications of key design options, of fee unobligated balances, and of approaches for managing revenue instability. For each of these three agencies, we reviewed agency annual reports and financial statements; we also reviewed agency fee collection procedures, policies, and data. We spoke with agency officials about their management of fee collections. To assess the reliability of OMB's MAX data, and data on unobligated balances that we received from FCC, we reviewed available documentation and followed up as needed to resolve any questions. Based on our review, we found these data sufficiently reliable for the purposes of our report.

To develop the key questions for managing revenue instability, we reviewed our past work on federal user fees—including our user fee design guide and reviews of specific fees—and considered our current audit work in the three selected agencies noted above. We also reviewed literature from governmental and nongovernmental organizations to identify common principles for managing reserve funds. Specifically, we used published guidance from a state government, from professional associations, and from a consulting firm that described practices in managing reserve funds; these sources were selected from a literature review, based upon their applicability to a federal fee-funded framework. Once we identified common themes in fee-funded programs that were experiencing revenue instability, and identified leading practices for creating and managing reserve funds, we developed a set of questions that agency managers and Congress could use to identify and manage fee revenue instability. We validated our key questions with subject matter specialists selected for their fee program expertise in both the public and private sectors, as well as with relevant officials at USPTO, the Mint, the FCC, and OMB.

We performed our work from August 2012 to September 2013 in accordance with generally accepted government auditing standards. Those standards require that we plan and perform the audit to obtain sufficient, appropriate evidence to provide a reasonable basis for our findings and conclusions based on our audit objectives. We believe that the evidence obtained provides a reasonable basis for our findings and conclusions based on our audit objectives.

BACKGROUND

In general, a user fee is related to some voluntary transaction or request for government goods or services, above and beyond what is normally available to the public (such as a national park entrance fee or a license to operate a radio station). We have previously reported on the characteristics (equity, efficiency, revenue adequacy, and administrative burden) that can influence the effectiveness of user fees to fund activities that provide benefits to identifiable users.[6]

User fee designs can vary widely and, in general, are governed by two authorities: an authority to charge fees, and an authority to use fee collections. Agencies derive their authority to charge fees either from the Independent Offices Appropriation Act of 1952 (IOAA) or from a specific statutory authority.[7] Overall, fees established under the IOAA must be (1) fair and (2) based on costs to the government, on the value of the service or thing to the recipient, on public policy, or on interest serviced. Agencies that established fees under the IOAA, however, are only authorized to charge the fee; a separate authority is required to use the fee collections. However, Congress has frequently provided agencies with the authority via authorizing or appropriations legislation both to collect fees and to use the collections. In these specific fee authorities, Congress determines the degree of flexibility to make fee design and implementation decisions that will be retained or delegated to the agency.

Regardless how the imposition of fee collections is authorized, Congressional action is required for agencies to use those collections. Congress may provide agencies with the authority to collect and use a fee within authorizing legislation, within appropriations legislation, or within both.[8] For agencies whose fee collections are available for obligation on a no-year or multi-year authority basis, unobligated balances can be carried forward from year to year. To illustrate the reasons why such balances exist in fee-related programs, we selected three fee-funded agencies with unobligated balances: the United States Mint (Mint), the United States Patent and Trademark Office (USPTO), and the Federal Communications Commission (FCC).

Table 1. Three Agencies Selected to Illustrate Reasons for Unobligated Balances in Fee Accounts

The United States Patent and Trademark Office (USPTO)	USPTO is a component of the Department of Commerce and is charged with examining applications and granting patents to new, useful, and non-obvious inventions and with reviewing and registering marks—trademarks, service marks, certification marks, and collective membership marks. USPTO is fully funded by fee collections paid by applicants and owners applying for and maintaining patents or trademarks. The fees correspond to products and services at different points in patent and trademark application and examination processes and lifecycles. The Leahy-Smith America Invents Act (AIA)[a] of 2011 provides USPTO the authority to set all fee amounts through the regulatory process. USPTO is authorized to spend the fee amounts collected each year, up to the amount appropriated by Congress. The AIA also created a special account called the Patent and Trademark Fee Reserve Fund, referred to as the FRF by USPTO. Any USPTO collections in excess of the amounts annually appropriated by Congress are deposited into this fund. The USPTO can access money from the Patent and Trademark Fee Reserve Fund only to the extent appropriated by Congress. We reported in 2012 that 90 percent of USPTO's revenues came from patent fees, and the remainder of revenue came from trademark fees.

Table 1. (Continued)

The United States Mint (Mint)	The Mint, a component of the Department of the Treasury, manufactures and distributes coins and medals. It provides circulating coins to the Federal Reserve for distribution to banks, and prepares and distributes numismatic items, including investment-grade bullion coins and high-quality versions of circulating coinage, precious metal coins, commemorative coins, medals, and sets. It is also responsible for safeguarding noncirculating coins and medals and the precious metals used to make them. In 1995, Congress created the United States Mint Public Enterprise Fund (PEF), which accounts for all receipts and expenses related to production and sale of numismatic items and circulating coinage, as well as protection activities. Since establishment of the PEF, the Mint has operated without direct appropriations, and is entirely funded by its collections. Any amounts in the PEF that are determined by the Mint to be in excess of the amount required for Mint expenses are transferred to the Treasury's General Fund. From fiscal years 2006 to 2010 the Mint returned collections between $388 million and $825 million annually to the General Fund. In fiscal year 2012 the Mint collected $3.4 billion in revenue from the sale of circulating and noncirculating items. Numismatic coins, including gold and silver bullion coins, generated approximately 86 percent of the Mint's revenues; sales of circulating coins generated 14 percent.
The Federal Communications Commission (FCC)	The FCC is an independent regulatory agency governed by five commissioners appointed by the President and confirmed by the Senate. It is charged with regulating interstate and international communications by radio, television, wire, satellite, and cable, and with regulating telecommunications services for all people of the United States. The FCC is authorized by Section 9 of the Communications Act of 1934 (as amended) to assess and collect regulatory fees to recover the regulatory costs associated with the Commission's enforcement, policy- and rulemaking, user information, and international

	activities;[b] it is subject to annual Congressional appropriations that specify the amount of regulatory fees it may collect each year. In addition, the FCC manages the Universal Service Fund (USF), which was created by the Telecommunications Act of 1996.[c] This fund is administered by the Universal Service Administrative Company (USAC), an independent, not-for-profit corporation designated as the administrator of the federal USF by the FCC, and financed by mandatory contributions from U.S. telecommunications service providers and other providers of telecommunications. The USAC provides USF funds directly to service providers to defray the cost of serving customers in high cost and rural areas, and of serving customers who have low incomes. In addition, USF funds provide financial support to assist schools, libraries, and health care providers in purchasing telecommunications services, advanced telecommunications and information services, and Internet access. In fiscal 2012, the FCC collected $340 million in the form of regulatory fees which were deposited into the FCC's salaries and expense account, and $9.3 billion in the form of contributions for the USF, which were deposited in the USF account administered by USAC.[d]

Source: USPTO, the Mint, and FCC.

Notes: (a) Leahy-Smith America Invents Act of 2011, P.L. 112-29. § 10 (Sept. 16, 2011).

(b) Pub. L. No. 73-416, section 9 is codified at 47 U.S.C. § 159. FCC also collects application fees from companies for activities such as license applications, renewals or requests for modification. These fees are deposited in the General Fund of the Treasury and cannot be used by the FCC. 47 U.S.C. § 158(e).

(c) Pub. L. No. 104-104, codified at 47 U.S.C. § 254.

(d) The remaining revenue collected was from contributions to the Telecommunications Relay Service Fund, and proceeds from radio spectrum auctions and the North American Numbering Plan.

FEE DESIGN AFFECTS THE BALANCE BETWEEN CONGRESSIONAL CONTROL AND AGENCY FLEXIBILITY AND HAS IMPLICATIONS FOR PROGRAM MANAGEMENT

Congress Delegates or Retains Varying Degrees of Decision-Making Authority Depending on How It Designs Key Aspects of User Fees

When designing fees, Congress is presented with a number of decisions regarding how a fee will be set, collected, used, and reviewed. At each decision point, Congress can delegate some flexibility to agencies, or it can retain that control. In the aggregate, these decisions enable Congress to design a fee that strikes its desired balance between agency flexibility and Congressional control. It is important to note that regardless of how Congress designs a fee, it always retains oversight over the fee and over the goods and services the fee supports. Figure 1 identifies six key fee design decisions for Congress that have a direct bearing on how much control Congress will retain and how much flexibility will be delegated to an agency.[9] For each design question, we have identified at least two options, one granting the agency more flexibility and the other retaining more control for Congress. In some cases, Congress selects an option that falls in between the two options shown in figure 1. For example, Congress can grant an agency the authority to set some of its fee rates by regulation while setting other fees, or requirements for any of the rates such as provisions for exemptions, waivers, and caps, in statute.

Fee Design Options Have Implications for Fee Program Management

Congress's fee design decisions have implications for fee program management beyond striking the desired balance between agency flexibility and Congressional control. Below, we discuss in more detail the key fee design options introduced in figure 1—setting, using, and reviewing—and the implications that flow from decisions about each design option. Understanding these implications, especially in the context of Congress's own priorities and goals, can help to avoid unintended consequences in fee design.

	Key design questions	Options increasing agency flexibility	Options increasing congressional control
Setting	How are fee rates set?	By regulation	In statute
Using	What Congressional action triggers the use of fee collections?	Offsetting collection authority	Offsetting receipt authority Government receipt authority
	What is the period of availability for the collections?	No year	Limited year
	For what purposes may the collections be used?	Broadly defined uses	Narrowly defined uses
	To what degree will Congress limit the amount of collections that can be used?	No limit	Limit set in statute
Reviewing	What types of reporting and oversight requirements are in place?	Basic requirements such as CFO Act Biennial Fee Reviews	Additional requirements

Source: GAO. [a]GAO-08-386SP.

Figure 1. Key Fee Design Decisions Allow for Agency Flexibility or Congressional Control. See Appendix I for additional information on Figure 1.

Implications of Fee Design: Setting

Figure 2 shows the key design options related to how fee rates are set.

	Key design questions	Options increasing agency flexibility	Options increasing congressional control
Setting	How are fee rates set?	By regulation	In statute

Source: GAO.

Note: See interactive figure on page 8 for more details.

Figure 2. Key Fee Design Options: Setting.

The frequency of fee review and adjustment, and the ability to keep fees and costs aligned, have a number of potential implications for agencies. The CFO Act[10] requires federal agencies to review user fees biennially and OMB's Circular A-25 directs agencies to set fees to recover all direct and indirect costs to the federal government of a good or service. We have previously reported that the failure to review fees regularly can result in large fee increases when the fees are eventually updated, which creates costly challenges.[11] For example, the U.S. Citizenship and Immigration Service (USCIS) is authorized to charge fees for the adjudication of immigration and naturalization applications. Although USCIS has the authority to adjust its fees through the regulatory process, in 2007 it conducted its first comprehensive fee review in nine years.[12] As a result, USCIS had to increase fees by an average of 86 percent to align them with its costs.[13] During the month before the fee increase took effect, the number of applications received increased an unprecedented 100 percent over the prior month, far outpacing the agency's processing capacity. This contributed to a backlog of 1.47 million applications and unplanned costs to secure additional facilities to store these applications. In 2012, we found that prior to the passage of the AIA, fees generating over 80 percent of the USPTO's revenues were set in statute.[14] This limited the USPTO's ability to adjust fee rates as costs changed. Other than periodic increases to reflect inflation, these statutorily-set fees had not been reviewed or adjusted for the 7 years before 2012.

In contrast, there are other examples of intentional deviation from cost-fee alignment. In some cases, a less precise alignment between costs and each fee is chosen in order to achieve a policy or administrative goal. A fully fee-funded agency covers program costs in the aggregate, but not necessarily on a fee-by-fee basis. For example, within the suite of USCIS's immigration and naturalization fees, Congress directed that fees providing adjudication and naturalization services be set to ensure recovery of full costs of providing such services. This includes the costs of similar services provided without charge to asylum applicants or other immigrants.[15] As a result, the costs of processing applicants granted the fee waivers are distributed to other fee payers as a flat-rate surcharge. However, unintentional misalignment between fees and costs can increase the demand for more expensive services, because fee payers do not bear the agency's total cost of the service. This can result in some fee payers subsidizing others with no public policy purpose.

We have found over the years that fees set through the regulatory process may be updated more frequently than fees set in statute: therefore, they may more consistently align collections with costs. 16 However, we have also previously reported that, in the past, stakeholders expressed concern about the agency incentive to inflate costs or the lack of incentive to restrain costs.[17] This risk may be reduced, and tools for Congressional and stakeholder oversight may be enhanced, if the agency clearly reports its methods for setting the fee, including an accounting of program costs and the assumptions it uses to project future program costs and fee collections. Further, federal agencies must also follow guidelines regarding their cost accounting information, providing some safeguards against artificial inflation of program costs.[18]

Implications of Fee Design: Using

Figure 3 shows the key design options related to an agency's access to and use of its fee collections.

Congressional decisions about the collection and use of a fee will determine how the fee will be considered within the context of all federal budgetary resources. Fee collections are classified into 3 categories: offsetting collections, offsetting receipts, or governmental receipts.[19] As noted in figure 1, fees classified as offsetting collections can provide agencies with more flexibility because they are generally available for agency obligation without an additional annual appropriation. In contrast, offsetting receipts and governmental receipts offer greater Congressional control because, generally, additional Congressional action is needed before the collections are available for agency obligation. Regular Congressional review—whether through reauthorization or the annual appropriations process—offers opportunities to exercise Congressional oversight. Regardless of the specific classification, all fees remain subject to Congressional oversight at any point in time.

	Key design questions	Options increasing agency flexibility	Options increasing congressional control
Using	What Congressional action triggers the use of fee collections?	Offsetting collection authority	Offsetting receipt authority Government receipt authority
	What is the period of availability for the collections?	No year	Limited year
	For what purposes may the collections be used?	Broadly defined uses	Narrowly defined uses
	To what degree will Congress limit the amount of collections that can be used?	No limit	Limit set in statute

Source: GAO.

Note: See interactive figure on page 8 for more details.

Figure 3. Key Fee Design Options: Using.

The authorities under which an agency may collect and use fees can be affected by different legislative decisions made over time, resulting in increased complexity and potentially significant intended or unintended effects. For example, a program's authorizing legislation may grant the agency the authority to collect fees but not provide the agency the authority to spend the fees. As a result, any later enacted legislation to allow the agency to spend the fees may not be consistent with the authorizing legislation, contributing to increased complexity.

Congress also determines the period of time the collections are available for obligation, the purposes for which they may be used, and the amount of collections that are available to the agency—thereby determining how much flexibility the agency has in managing its fee collections.

Time

When Congress limits the period of availability of funds, it retains greater control over when the funds will be used. When Congress provides an agency unlimited access to its fee collections (that is, makes the fee collections available until they are expended) agencies have greater flexibility and can carry over unobligated amounts to future fiscal years. This enables agencies to align fees and costs over a longer horizon and to better prepare for, and adjust to, fluctuations in collections and costs. Carrying over unobligated balances from year to year, if an agency has multi- or no-year fee collections, is one way a reserve can be established. Set aside or reserved funds can sustain operations in the event of a sharp downturn in collections or increase in costs. We have previously found that, for programs where fees are expected to cover all or most program costs, and especially when program costs do not necessarily decline with a drop in fee collections, a reserve is important.[20]

(Later in this report, we will discuss reserve funds at fee-funded agencies.)

Purpose

Congress can also specify limits on the activities or purposes for which an agency may use fee collections. Congress has granted some agencies broad authority to use some of the fees they collect for any program purpose, but has limited the use of other fees to specific sets of activities. Such restrictions may benefit stakeholders and increase Congressional control. For example, according to USPTO officials, patent fee collections can only be used for patent processes, and trademark fee collections can only be used for trademark processes, as well as the proportionate share of the administrative costs of the agency. USPTO officials stated that patent and trademark customers are typically two distinct groups and this division helps to assure stakeholders that their fees are supporting the activities that affect them directly.

On the other hand, statutes that too narrowly limit how fees can be used reduces both Congress's flexibility to make resource decisions and an agency's flexibility to reallocate resources. This can make it more difficult to pursue public policy goals or respond to changing program needs, such as when the activities intended to achieve fee-funded purposes change. For example, Customs and Border Protection's (CBP) Merchandise Processing Fee is authorized to fund only a specific set of activities. However, after the events of September 11, 2001, as the program's focus shifted towards security, other activities (such as screening and inspecting conveyances and inspecting vessels and containers) became part of the program. While CBP views these activities as part of the merchandise processing service, they are not included in the set of authorized activities that may be funded by the fee collections; the result is a misalignment between the services provided and the authorized uses for the fees.

Narrowing the authorized uses of a fee in statute can also increase agency administrative costs. For example, the narrower the subset of activities for which collections can be used, the more detailed and potentially expensive the required cost accounting. Given these challenges, more frequent reviews and updated fee schedules become even more important to ensure that the authorized purposes remain aligned with program needs. For example, in 2008 we reported that some CBP inspection fees can pay for only some inspection activities and only under certain circumstances. In order to be reimbursed for time spent on authorized activities for various fees, CBP must track the time spent on these activities for several of its inspection fees—including customs,

immigration, and agriculture activities.[21] In early 2007, to help address a concern that timekeeping was taking time away from officers' inspection duties, CBP implemented a standard process for tracking the time dedicated for these activities. However, at one port we visited for the 2008 report, on each shift, a full-time CBP officer was assigned solely to tracking staff time. In 2013, we found that CBP still does not capture all of the time spent on agriculture activities in its Cost Management Information System—the system in which CBP tracks its activities and determines personnel costs.[22]

Amount

Congress determines the specific level of budget authority provided for a program's activities by limiting the amount of fee collections that can be collected or used by the agency; however, these limits can also pose challenges for the agency. For example, when the agency is not authorized to retain or use all of its fee collections and no other funding source is provided, the agency may not have the funds available to produce the goods or services that it has promised, or that it is required by law to provide. In a 2012 report, we found that in USPTO's case, fees must be designed to recover costs of the related activities in aggregate as directed by the AIA.[23] However, with each set of application fees collected, USPTO takes on an additional work activity. In some years Congress chose not to make available to USPTO the full amount of its collections to support that work.[24] USPTO officials stated that, prior to the passage of the AIA, this contributed to USPTO's inability to hire sufficient examiners to keep up with USPTO's workload and invest in needed technology systems to modernize the USPTO. In 2012, we reported a backlog of over 640,000 patent applications.[25]

Limiting the availability of fee collections may also have future budgetary implications for Congress. For example, as mentioned above, USPTO collections in excess of appropriations are deposited into the Patent and Trademark Fee Reserve Fund and are not available to the agency without additional Congressional action. If these amounts are made available in future years rather than in the year the fees were collected, the action will count or "score" as new budget authority against discretionary spending limits in place in a given future fiscal year, and will not offset against budget authority made available that year. The effect of this scoring may make the fee-funded activities appear more costly and can make granting access to previously collected amounts a less desirable option for Congressional fee designers. The outcome can lead to the buildup of unavailable and unobligated balances.

Implications of Fee Design: Reviewing

Figure 4 shows the design decisions related to the kinds of specific reporting or review requirements Congress may wish to impose, beyond the standard biennial review requirement in the CFO Act.

	Key fee design questions	Options increasing agency flexibility or responsibility	Options increasing congressional control or oversight
Reviewing	What types of reporting and oversight requirements are in place?	Basic requirements such as CFO Act Biennial Fee Reviews	Additional requirements

Source: GAO.

Note: See interactive figure on page 8 for more details.

Figure 4. Key Fee Design Options: Reviewing.

When designing a fee, Congress must balance granting more autonomy to an agency (by requiring no additional reporting and review beyond that required in the CFO Act) with stronger control for itself (via additional reporting and oversight requirements over and above the CFO Act requirements). When a fee's authorizing statute does not specify review and reporting requirements or if a fee derives its statutory authority from the Independent Offices Appropriation Act of 1952,[26] the CFO Act requires and OMB Circular No. A-25 directs agencies to review their fees biennially and to recommend fee adjustments as appropriate. In addition, OMB Circular No. A-25 directs agencies to include non-fee-funded programs in these reviews to determine whether fees should be initiated for government services or goods for which fees are not currently charged. Further, if imposing such fees is prohibited or restricted by law, agencies are to recommend legislative changes as appropriate. Moreover, OMB Circular No. A-25 directs agencies to discuss the results of these reviews and any resulting proposals, such as adjustments to fee rates, in annual reports, such as performance and accountability reports. However, our 2011 survey of the 24 agencies covered by the CFO Act and OMB Circular No. A-25 suggested that agencies are reviewing more fees than they are discussing in their annual reports.[27] While these reviews may provide information for agency management and decision making, the extent to which this information is being shared with Congressional decision makers or other stakeholders appears far more limited. In 2012, we concluded that OMB should do more to ensure that agencies comply with requirements and recommended that OMB use its budget reviews to ensure agencies are adhering to this guidance. As of March 2013, OMB had not taken action on this recommendation.[28]

Additional reporting requirements can further increase information available to Congress about fee programs. We previously concluded that whether fee rates are set by the agency in regulation or by Congress in statute, agencies must substantively review and report on all cost-based fees regularly to ensure decision makers have complete information about program costs and activities.[29] A variety of reporting requirements can be included in appropriations, authorizing legislation, or committee reports. For example, AIA requires USPTO to report on the implementation of the AIA, which includes fee-setting authority. In addition, USPTO's 2012 appropriations required a spending plan to access funds in the Patent and Trademark Fee Reserve Fund. Similarly, the Mint is required to report to Congress biennially on the status of coin production costs, and annually on the operation of the Mint's Numismatic Public Enterprise Fund, as well as provide quarterly financial reports on the Funds.

Reporting requirements sometimes contain requirements to include stakeholders during the course of reviews. For example, in accordance with the AIA, USPTO is required to work with the relevant public advisory committee to hold public hearings on fee-setting, to consider and analyze any comments, advice or recommendations from the advisory committee, and to publish proposed and final rules in the *Federal Register*, including the purpose, rationale, and possible benefits resulting from the change. Our previous work has found that including stakeholders in the fee review process can increase success for substantive, two-way communication and understanding/buy-in on the fee setting process,[30] and that effectively communicating with stakeholders involves sharing relevant analysis and information as well as providing opportunities for stakeholder input.[31]

Agencies Manage Unobligated Balances Differently Depending on Whether They Represent Operating Reserves or Reflect the Timing of Collections and Outlays

Identifying and understanding unobligated balances in fee-based accounts is challenging. There is no single list of all federal user fees. In addition, although some fees are deposited into an account containing only fee collections, others are deposited into accounts that also contain other types of funds such as general fund appropriations. In general, budget accounts are not labeled in a way that indicates whether the account contains fee collections. This also makes it challenging to identify which unobligated balances in an account are related to fee collections. Further, as discussed below, some fee designs include dedicated reserves that appear as unobligated balances. Despite these challenges, unobligated balances must be carefully monitored in agencies funded by fee collections.

Table 2. Unobligated Balances of Selected Fee-Funded Agencies, Fiscal Year 2012

	USPTO	Mint	FCC
Unobligated balance	$238 million	$694 million	$3.2 billion
Total budget authority	$2.4 billion	$3.4 billion	$10.5 billion
Unobligated balances as a percentage of budget authority	9.9%	20.4%	30.5%

Source: GAO review of agency financial reports and GAO calculation.

The three fee-funded agencies took different approaches to managing their unobligated balances. At the end of the fiscal years 2009 through 2012, USPTO, the Mint, and the FCC each reported large unobligated balances related to fee collections (see table 2). The origin of each agency's unobligated balance, and how each agency manages its unobligated balance, is related in part to how the fees were designed by Congress and the agencies.

U.S. Patent and Trademark Office's Unobligated Balances Are a Long-Term Strategy to Manage Revenue Instability

USPTO's $238 million unobligated balance at the end of fiscal year 2012 represents the agency's operating reserve. USPTO officials said that during the economic recession in fiscal year 2009, the agency experienced serious operational challenges as a result of a decline in the number of applications and patent renewals – and corresponding fee collections.[32] When collections are less than costs, USPTO faces a situation which impairs its ability to maintain operations, hire sufficient examiners, and invest in technology to handle a large backlog (approximately 591,000 patent applications as of July 2013). In 2010, to smooth the impact of economic downturns on operations and to help address funding uncertainty, USPTO announced its intention to designate a portion of Congress's annual appropriations as an operating reserve that could be carried over for use in future years. This reserve appears in USPTO's financial statements and OMB's budget database as an unobligated balance. USPTO officials said they do not intend to obligate these funds unless needed, and therefore USPTO will likely report unobligated balances every year. This operating reserve is separate and distinct from the Patent and Trademark Fee Reserve Fund established by the AIA, which is only available to USPTO to the extent appropriated by Congress and currently has no balance.[33]

In its patent fee rulemaking process, USPTO established and communicated a strategy to its stakeholders for developing the agency's patent operating reserve. In its proposed and final rules, USPTO included information on the intended size and funding strategy for the reserve. While developing this strategy, USPTO also sought and incorporated stakeholder input. For example, in response to comments from the public and from the Patent Public Advisory Committee, USPTO decided to slow the reserve's growth and to reduce the amount of fees designated for the reserve beginning in fiscal year 2013. In fiscal year 2013, USPTO issued a final rule reflective of this input and increased its patent fees, in part to fund a 3 month operating reserve (approximately $700 million) by fiscal year 2018. Specifically, the final rule adopted fees set at a lower amount compared to the proposed rule.

To determine the size of its reserve, USPTO used a risk assessment process to inform its decision-making, analyzing its operations and drawing on the reserve guidance from other organizations.[34] The two main factors that contribute to instability in patent operations are increases in costs and decreases in fee collections. Costs of patent operations consist mostly of the expense of patent examinations, and also include expenditures for information technology and general support costs. Collections consist of fees paid by patent applicants at different stages of the examination process and throughout the life of the patent: they vary with the speed of the application process (which is a function of the number of examiners available), and with economic conditions both in the United States and in other countries. USPTO plans to assess the patent operating reserve balance against its target balance annually and, at least every 2 years, plans to evaluate whether the target balance is sufficient to meet USPTO's needs. According to agency officials, a similar reserve is planned for trademark fees, but the analysis to determine the appropriate size of the reserve is on-going; USPTO officials expect this analysis to be completed in fiscal year 2014.

The Mint's Unobligated Balance Represents a Reserve to Address Policy Changes, Collection Declines and Increased Costs

The Mint's unobligated balance is the source of the Mint's operating reserves, established in 2011 in response to operational challenges. Specifically, Mint officials said that they regularly review their open obligations, liabilities, projected earnings, and financial risks which include not having sufficient cash to meet required obligations, or sufficient resources needed to fulfill the mission appropriately. The Mint has had to take into account various factors, including (1) a decline in the Federal Reserve's demand for circulating coins due to the recession, (2) the Treasury Secretary's decision to suspend minting and issuing of $1 coins for circulation, (3) an increase in metal prices causing the Mint to lose money on the production of one-cent and 5-cent coins, (4) delays in release of numismatic products for sale, (5) decreasing demand for the Mint's numismatic products, and (6) increasing demand for the cash-intensive silver bullion coin program.

In response to these factors, Mint officials exercised their authority to suspend transfers of collections from the Mint's circulating coin revenues to the General Fund and, starting in fiscal year 2011, reserves were created from the unobligated balance as follows:

- Seignorage Reserve ($377.5 million as of August 2013): established to approximate one year's worth of circulating coinage operating expenses. This is to ensure continued delivery of coinage to the Federal Reserve Banks until other mitigating decisions or strategies are implemented to offset any effects that are impairing the continued financing of circulating operations
- Numismatic Reserve ($50 million as of August 2013): established to mitigate the risk of loss in revenue in sufficient amounts to cover cost should demand significantly decrease. The reserve represents the availability of funds for ongoing funding of approximately one year's funding of the Mint's protection activity. The protection activity is a cost without revenue to offset, and presents the most significant cost to fully cover should demand significantly decrease.

Mint officials said they will to continue to monitor Mint operations and the operating environment, including changes in customer demand, costs of inputs, administration policies, natural or man-made disasters, and critical investment needs, to determine if the reserves are at suitable levels for their purposes. These target levels were set at a level meant to reflect the needs and/or the risks that require mitigation over the next 2-5 years.

Federal Communications Commission's Unobligated Balance Largely Reflects the Timing of Collections and Outlays

Both FCC's salaries and expenses account, which contains regulatory fee collections, and USAC's USF contribution account had unobligated balances at the end of fiscal year 2012, with the USF account,[35] which includes Telecommunications Relay Service funds, containing much larger unobligated balances (approximately $3 billion) than the salaries and expenses account ($18 million). According to FCC officials, $10.4 million in unobligated funds in the salaries and expenses account is no-year funding and will be reapportioned in fiscal year 2013. Of the remaining $7.6 million, FCC officials said that $7.1 million will remain unobligated until FCC receives OMB and

Congressional approval for special projects, and $500,000 relates to expired reimbursable authority. According to FCC officials, the salaries and expenses account's unobligated balances were regulatory fees associated with expired contracts or Recovery Act funds deobligated because contracts had not been signed.

Since fiscal year 2008, the FCC has not been provided access to its regulatory fee collections in excess of its annual appropriation. FCC's annual appropriation permits the agency to assess and collect regulatory fees up to a specified amount. This amount remains available until expended. 36 With respect to USF contributions, FCC officials reported that the approximately $3 billion in unobligated balances from USAC's USF amounts[37] was largely the result of the timing of collections and obligations for the four programs funded by USF contributions: (1) the Connect America Fund (also known as the High Cost program) for rural areas, (2) the Lifeline program (for low-income consumers), (3) the Schools and Libraries (or E-rate) program, and (4) the Rural Health Care program.[38] A significant length of time can lapse between contribution collections and the funding commitment. In the E-rate and Rural Health Care programs, the USAC does not record USF amounts as committed until the application is approved.

In addition to these timing issues, FCC officials said some USF contributions are set aside for specific multi-year pilot projects and appeals. Table 3 below shows the contributions, disbursements, and amounts set-aside in each program for fiscal 2012.

Table 3. Collections, Disbursements, and Set-Asides for Universal Service Fund Programs, 2012

	Connect America	Schools and libraries	Rural health care	Lifeline
Contributions received (CY)	$4.5 billion	$2.4 billion	$110 million	$2.3 billion
Disbursements to providers (CY)	$4.1 billion	$2.3 billion	$173.5 million	$2.0 billion
Unobligated balance (FY)	$ 1 billion	$1.7 billion	$136 million	$205 million
Reserves/set-asides (FY)	$805 million (for Connect America Fund implementation)	$683 million (for appeals and invoice extension requests)		$25 million (for broadband pilot)

Source: FCC

Considering Key Questions About Costs and Collections Can Enable Congress and Agencies to Identify and Manage Revenue Instability

The more a program or agency depends on fees to fund its activities, the more vulnerable it is to revenue instability: that is, the extent to which fee collections cover the intended share of costs over time.[39] Largely or wholly fee-funded programs do not necessarily see a proportional decline in costs when they experience a drop in collections. Absent access to other funding sources these program are sensitive to revenue instability, making the following considerations especially important.[40]

Key aspects of fee design can help or hinder agencies in managing revenue instability, and minimize or exacerbate the effect on the agency's ability to provide goods or services. The following key questions center on understanding (1) the data and analysis needed to identify and manage revenue instability, (2) the factors likely to affect collections, (3) the factors likely to affect costs, and (4) how agencies can manage fee revenue instability. They will be most useful when considered in conjunction with key questions for designing and implementing user fees: that is, how fees are set, collected, used and reviewed.[41] Appendix II provides a summary of the key questions discussed below.

What Data and Analysis are Needed to Identify and Manage Revenue Instability?

In order to identify and manage revenue instability, decision makers need regular information and analysis to understand potential vulnerabilities in the context of the specific fee design. The authority to create or implement a tool to manage revenue instability may be retained by Congress or it may be delegated to the agency. But regardless of where the authority lies, it is the agency's responsibility to obtain and analyze the necessary data to inform decision making. This is true even—or especially—in cases where statutory authority is required to act on the analysis.

Agencies should consider the following questions when gathering information for decision makers.

What is the risk that fee revenue instability will affect this program?

In considering approaches to managing fee revenue instability, an agency should develop a risk-based strategy. Risk assessment is the identification and analysis of relevant risks associated with achieving the program's objectives, and with forming a basis for determining how risks should be managed. Risk identification methods may include qualitative and quantitative ranking activities, management conferences, forecasting and strategic planning, and findings from audits and other reviews.

Once risks have been identified, they should be analyzed for their possible effect. Risk analysis generally includes estimating the risk's significance, assessing the likelihood of its occurrence, and deciding how to manage the risk. GAO's *Standards for Internal Controls in the Federal Government* notes that the specific risk analysis methodology used can vary by agency because of differences in agencies' missions and the difficulty in qualitatively and quantitatively assigning risk levels.[42]

The strategy developed to manage revenue instability should match the level of risk identified. For example, preparing for risks that are highly unlikely but would have dire consequences can result in a reserve balance that is unnecessarily high and draws revenue away from other fee program needs. In 2013, we found that for the Agricultural Quarantine Inspection (AQI) program, the Animal and Plant Health Inspection Service (APHIS) had based its target reserve balance on largely unrealistic risks—including the possibility of ceasing all inspections—and as a result, developed a target reserve balance that was unnecessarily high.[43] We recommended a reserve target that is more closely aligned with program needs and risks. United States Department of Agriculture agreed with the recommendation, and adjusted its target reserve balance to a level it said would allow for continuous services in the event of an unforeseen decrease in user fee collections, or other instances that could cause an increase in workload for the program.

What analysis should be performed and what data are needed?

The appropriate analysis can help an agency obtain a thorough understanding of factors such as cost drivers and elements that influence collections. As recognized in the *Statement of Federal Financial Accounting Standards 4: Managerial Cost Accounting Standards and Concepts*, agency cost information should be sufficient to be used by Congress and federal executives in making program and resources decisions, as well as for setting fees, but the analysis does not necessarily need to be complex, costly, or require special resources. Agencies should seek to leverage data and analysis that already exists. For example, agencies may use proxies, or leading or lagging indicators to forecast key changes, rather than undertake complex, original analysis to do the same. USCIS is almost entirely funded from immigration and naturalization application fees and uses data from DHS's Office of Immigration Statistics, among other sources, to project the volume of incoming applications.[44]

Are there limitations to the available data (such as preliminary estimates) that could add uncertainty to collection estimates?

Indicators that are drawn from early estimates may add vulnerabilities to demand or collection forecasts. For example, each quarter, Universal Service Administrative Company projects the next quarter's anticipated USF demand and assessable industry revenues. The FCC uses this information to determine the applicable contribution factor (percentage of assessable revenues) for the following quarter. FCC officials have found that their use of projected data in setting the USF contribution factor has led to collections that are more or less than initially expected.

How frequently should this analysis be conducted?

Once the necessary analysis has been identified, agencies should consider how frequently to perform the analysis. Although agencies are required to conduct biennial fee reviews per the CFO Act, revenue instability may occur over a shorter time horizon and may demand more frequent examinations. In particular, agencies should balance informational and reporting needs with the cost of performing the analysis. For example, FCC reviews USF outlays, receipts, and cash balances monthly, and these are taken into account in the quarterly adjustment of the USF contribution factor.

What Factors Could Affect the Timing and Pattern of Collections?

Fee-funded agencies sometimes experience revenue instability as a result of how, or how frequently, fees are collected and external factors that can influence the demand for the goods or services. Agencies can plan for contingencies by understanding the factors affecting payers and external events affecting the collection process. Asking the following questions could help decision makers plan for contingencies.

How frequently are fees collected?

User fees are not always received at regular or predictable intervals throughout the year. The frequency of collections is sometimes related to how and by whom fees are collected and paid to the Treasury. For example, airlines collect international air passenger inspection fees at the time a ticket is sold, but remit fees to the government quarterly on behalf of the passengers. Collections that come in small increments on a rolling basis or late in the fiscal year may inhibit an agency's ability to identify patterns and fluctuations in collections in the aggregate, or may create cash flow challenges. For example, USCIS receives application fees throughout the fiscal year but enters into year-long contracts at the start of the fiscal year. Because of the kind of legal authority USCIS has to obligate funds, USCIS must have collections equal to the full contract value available for obligation at the start of the year. (See also: What is the timing and pattern of spending?)

What remittance compliance issues may exist, and what are the tools for ensuring compliance?

Agencies may not collect amounts they are owed because of external factors affecting payers or because of vulnerabilities in the remittance process. For example, the FCC adjusts contribution rates and payments due from telecommunication service providers quarterly; however, abrupt changes in a company's finances (such as bankruptcy) can affect the actual remittance amounts. On the other hand, CBP has lost an unknown amount of revenue because it does not verify that it collects applicable user fees for every commercial truck, private aircraft, and private vessel for which the fees are due.[45]

In the event payers do not remit fees in a timely manner, the agency may need tools such as penalties to ensure remittance compliance. For example, CBP can levy interest charges or deny landing rights to airlines for non- or late remittance of the international air passenger inspection fees.[46] Similarly, the FCC can place a delinquent payer of regulatory user fees or USF contributions in "Red Light" status, which results in withholding Commission action in any licensing or similar proceeding until the payment or other satisfactory arrangements are made.

What external known or unknown events could affect fee collections?

Understanding external influences – for example, weather, world events, or changes in technology— allows for the proper planning of resources or the use of limited funding in the face of changing revenue. For example, according to USPTO officials, economic activity, like a recession, is an important consideration when developing workload forecasts, primarily patent and trademark application filings. In addition to economic factors, officials stated that USPTO considers overseas activity, policies and legislation, process efficiencies, and anticipated applicant behavior when preparing estimates. Estimates of incoming workload are developed after researching and modeling these elements, which helps USPTO plan. There may be indirect influences as well. For example, a fee on imports may be tied to the exchange rate. When currency exchange rates are favorable, the demand for cheaper items from foreign countries may increase. In this example the fee revenue would go up, or conversely, it would go down with a weaker exchange rate. Programs should regularly conduct environmental scans to identify new influences, or significant changes to existing influences.

Program management decisions can also influence the level of demand for a fee-funded activity, for example, when services are delivered through a third party. In 2010, we found that FCC had allowed certain prepaid wireless providers to be eligible telecommunications carriers in order to expand the availability of its Lifeline program.[47] Both participation in the program and payments to providers increased, but the program's internal controls were not addressing the risks of the telecommunication providers' inconsistent adherence to applicant eligibility requirements.[48]

In programs where fees for some activities subsidize the costs for other activities, payers' overuse of the subsidized activity may affect the agency's ability to cover costs. For example, according to USPTO officials, USPTO has intentionally designed fees to encourage innovation by reducing up-front fees for patent applicants and imposing higher maintenance fees later in the process, after users have already obtained a patent. Moreover, higher than aggregate costs must be charged of applicants and owners that do not qualify for reduced fees as a small or micro entity applicant. However, if applicants pay only the lower application filing fee and then decide against maintaining the patent, the higher maintenance fees are lost to USPTO. Because USPTO incurs the same cost to process an application whether the patent is maintained or not, and because costs are fully recovered in the aggregate over time and not at each step in the patent process, USPTO's patent examination costs do not match collections if maintenance fees are not collected.

How quickly is a change in collection amounts likely to occur?

External events or changes to internal policies can affect collections, in either the short or long term. For example, USPTO officials said rates of collections can change rapidly in response to economic events. During the 2009 recession, fewer patent applications were filed and maintained than were anticipated in the 2009 fiscal year, which reduced fee collections. Policy changes can affect collections as well, as when USCIS experienced a 100 percent increase in immigration and naturalization applications before USCIS increased its fees by an average of 86 percent in July 2007. Revenues can also be affected by market supply and demand. Further analysis can reveal whether fee changes are prudent based on the price elasticity of the good or service being provided, including whether there may be substitutes in the private sector.[49]

What Factors Can Affect Costs in Fee-funded Programs?

Fee-funded agencies should ask the following questions to gather information about the factors that affect their costs.

What are the fixed and variable costs of fee-funded activities?

If a fee is designed to recover all or a portion of the costs associated with an agency program or service, it is critical that agencies record, accumulate, and analyze timely and reliable data relating to those costs, consistent with applicable federal cost accounting standards. For example, according to USPTO officials, when USPTO began redesigning its fees under AIA in 2011, it used an activity-based cost accounting system to understand all agency costs as they relate to the activities performed supporting the fees collected. USPTO's Activity Based Information helps officials identify and analyze current activity costs on an ongoing basis, which helps with planning decisions as well as justifying budget requests.

What is the timing and pattern of spending?

Program management needs to understand the timing of program obligations in relation to the timing of collections during the fiscal year. As with collections, some agencies may have predictable patterns of obligations — whether regularly scheduled payments (such as payroll) or established spikes at particular points in the year (such as payouts for performance awards or bonuses). Other obligations may occur in a less predictable pattern.

Large upfront costs (such as IT investments or capital asset purchases) should be identified in time to capture those costs when setting fee rates, especially if the costs are ongoing (see also: *Develop and Maintain a Reserve Fund*). Fee-funded programs may require specific efforts to ensure that necessary infrastructure improvements are not neglected in cost accounting methods. For example, in 2007, USCIS stated in its fee review its intention to use all premium-processing fee collections toward investments in information technology and business-system transformation,[50] two planned infrastructure improvements.[51]

Can the agency quickly respond to changing costs?

Fee-funded programs may have flexibility to adjust program activities in response to rising costs, but certain types of costs create vulnerabilities if not considered in advance. For example, if fee-funded activities are inherently governmental in nature, and therefore required to be performed by federal employees, a reduction in fee revenue may be more challenging, because it takes longer to increase or decrease the number of federal employees than it would to adjust the number of contractors.

Data analysis can help program managers understand how quickly changes in costs could affect program activities. For example, USF sometimes experiences short-term changes in demand, stemming from program changes (such as the creation of pilot programs), revised eligibility rules, or program growth due to outreach efforts. The FCC and USAC regularly monitor potential changes in the level of USF commitments, and calculate the telecommunication companies' contribution levels on a quarterly basis. This allows USF collections to be more responsive to mid-year changes in obligations.

What is the relationship between costs and revenue?

Without data analysis, it is difficult to fully understand the relationship between costs and revenue. If costs increase and there is no corresponding increase in collections, programs will likely experience a cost-collections gap that needs to be addressed. However, increasing costs are sometimes due to improvements in service delivery (which can be more expensive), and over the course of time may lead to increased revenue. For example, a USPTO official said that spending more on overtime can increase production, which in this case is increasing the number of patent applications being examined. Since fees are required for many responses during examination, the increase in overtime costs generates more fee revenue as a result of the increase in applications examined and the replies necessary.

Decision Makers Can Manage Revenue Instability By More Closely Aligning Fees and Costs and Using Reserve Funds

To manage revenue instability actively and ensure continuity of goods or services, fee-funded agencies can better align fees with costs and create reserve funds. First, ensuring that program costs and fee rates remain aligned will minimize the chance of a cost-collections gap over the longterm. If revenue instability is a function of a fee's design, the most sustainable solutions will be found by realigning costs and collections. Not all fee revenue instability can be completely addressed in this way, however, and some agencies may need to take additional action. Maintaining a reserve can help address sudden or temporary fluctuations in collections and/or costs, and can minimize the effect of revenue instability on operations. Reserve funds can both help manage revenue instability, and where appropriate, serve as a mechanism for accumulating revenue for identified future capital investments.

Closer Alignment of Fee Costs and Collections

To determine whether closer cost-collection alignment could sufficiently and timely address revenue instability, agencies should consider the following questions.

How quickly can the program adjust fee rates in response to changes in collections or costs?

Adjusting fees through either statutory or rulemaking processes can be a lengthy process, so it is important to plan ahead. Regular fee reviews ensure that Congress, stakeholders, and agencies have complete information about changing costs and whether a fee needs to be changed.

Are fees set at a rate that enables the program to respond to spikes or surges?

Fee reviews can help agencies determine if they are prepared for spikes or surges in demand, which may occur more or less frequently, depending on the good or service. Over-staffing or excess capital creates waste and establishes a higher-than-needed unit cost for the service; however 100 percent efficiency provides for no flexibility to address surge capacity.

Does the program have other sources of funding that may mitigate initial revenue shortfalls, or is the program fully fee-reliant?

Fully fee-funded programs typically experience some lag time before initial collections are realized. To cover costs before collections are realized, the program may require another source of initial funding. Congress has sometimes provided this initial funding through an appropriation that may or may not be reimbursed over time. If an appropriation is to be reimbursed, reimbursement is generally done through incoming fee collections.

Develop and Maintain a Reserve Fund

When the risks of revenue instability are greater than the agency can manage by aligning costs and fees, having a reserve can enable the agency to continue providing goods and services despite fluctuations in collections, and to act quickly in response to changing conditions. Reserve funds can also be a tool for fee-funded programs in planning for capital investments. Agencies should consider the following questions in developing a reserve fund.

What legal authority does the program or agency have to develop and fund a reserve?

Before an agency commits to building a reserve, agencies must understand their statutory structures. Agencies with no-year funds—that is, collections that remain available for obligation until expended – allowing the agency to carry over balances indefinitely. This gives the agency the flexibility to build or maintain an internal reserve fund within their existing fee accounts. Also, agencies with multiyear collections, or collections available for obligation for a fixed period of time beyond one fiscal year, may also be able to maintain a reserve fund. Absent those authorities, agencies would require additional authority from Congress to develop and maintain a reserve. If not specified in statute, agencies should verify their legal authority to keep funds in reserve.

Further, individual authorizing statutes may require or restrict a fee reserve. For example, the Consolidated Omnibus Reconciliation Act of 1985 (COBRA) requires CBP to maintain a $30 million reserve in the existing COBRA fee account, and the United States Department of Agriculture's AQI program is authorized to develop and maintain a fee reserve in the existing fee account.

Does the agency need to notify Congress or seek permission, beyond its existing authority, to use its reserve fund?

Money in the reserve may only be accessible up to a set amount or within a specified time frame. Decision makers can also limit use of the reserve in other ways, such as

- money in the reserve may only be available for specified purposes or in response to a trigger, like a natural disaster;
- agencies may only have access to reserves in specific amounts, such as a percentage at a time in order to avoid total depletion of funds, or
- agencies may be required to report on their level of use and their plan for ending their use of the reserve.

Alternative budget account structures like a reimbursable account or revolving fund could help mitigate budgeting or timing challenges without compromising accountability for federal funds.[52] Program managers may also consider what mechanisms exist within the agency to track reserve balances.

What is the goal of the reserve?

Regardless of the authority under which a reserve is created, setting clear goals for the reserve and clarifying how the reserve will be implemented helps ensure accountability and transparency both to Congress and users of fee-based programs. For example, some agencies may wish to use a reserve to help ensure the long-term financial stability of the agency or to position the agency to respond to varying economic conditions. Others may seek a reserve to smooth expected fluctuations in costs or collections, or to build capital for necessary infrastructure improvements.

Still other programs may seek a reserve as a means to mitigate unforeseen and unavoidable revenue shortfalls.

Historical data can demonstrate to Congress, to stakeholders, and to fee payers why a reserve is needed. For example, based on USPTO's experience with a rapid decline in collections during the recession in 2009, and to address other sources of revenue instability, officials told us they are building an operating reserve to avoid a slowdown in operations should collections suddenly decline. According to officials, the agency used risk assessments of spending levels and revenue streams to explain to stakeholders why fees were being increased to build an operating reserve. (See also: *What is the risk that revenue instability will affect this program?*)

Who should review and approve the reserve policy?

In addition to notifying Congress as part of a transparent communication strategy, reserve policies could be published and reviewed by stakeholders via the *Federal Register* notice and comment process or alternatively, by existing fee advisory boards or committees. Internal agency policies may also require review by cognizant financial officers.

What level of reserves should be maintained?

To ensure accountability and adherence to the reserve's goals, establishing minimum and maximum reserve levels may be advisable. These numbers should be justified with program data and risk management considerations. When established reserve goals have been achieved, such as to fund planned capital investments, the level of reserve should be assessed for reasonableness.

How should the reserve fund be built and at what pace?

Data analysis and communication with users should inform the rate at which funds are applied to the reserve, and what actions are taken when the desired level is reached. For example, USPTO estimated in January 2013 that the patent operating reserve would reach its target of 3 months of operating expenses in fiscal year 2018, after accumulating a proportion of patent fees over 5 years. As the operating reserve approaches its target, USPTO plans to consider the level of reserve in its biennial fee review. USPTO sought input from patent users and stakeholders in creating a reasonable timeline for building its reserve.

CONCLUDING OBSERVATIONS

In 2012, the President's budget reported collections of nearly $300 billion in federal user fees, funding a wide variety of programs integral to our nation's security, to the security of our financial system, and to the protection of our natural resources. In light of the nation's current fiscal condition, it is essential that every funding source and spending decision be carefully considered and applied to its best and most efficient use. By their nature, federal user fees do not—and should not—follow a single model or design. However, wide variation can contribute to more challenging oversight. In light of this, it is critical for Congress and agencies to understand the implications of the key design decisions— each choice in isolation and also in the aggregate—to achieve a deliberate design that minimizes unintended consequences. Regardless of the fee design decisions made, Congress and agencies both have a role in effectively managing fee funded programs and ensuring that fees are designed to meet the goals of the program and are managed effectively.

The same prudent management standards should be applied to fee-funded programs as to those funded by general revenues. As such, unobligated balances in fee programs should be scrutinized. The federal budget's accounting structure can make it challenging to isolate unobligated balances resulting from fee collections, increasing the responsibility agencies have to manage and report on unobligated fee balances. Unobligated balances in fee programs may represent a reserve intended to manage the effects of revenue instability. However, to be effective as a reserve, agencies and Congress need to understand a fee's vulnerabilities and be deliberate in their design of a reserve fund to effectively manage them.

AGENCY COMMENTS & OUR EVALUATION

We provided a draft of this report for review and comment to the Secretaries of Commerce and Treasury, and the Managing Director of the Federal Communications Commission (FCC). The Secretary of Commerce and the Managing Director of the FCC provided technical changes, which we incorporated where appropriate. We also provided a copy of the report to the Office of Management and Budget.

Sincerely yours,

Susan J. Irving
Director for Federal Budget Analysis
Strategic Issues

Jacqueline M. Nowicki
Acting Director
Education, Workforce, and Income Security

APPENDIX I: KEY FEE DESIGN DECISIONS ALLOW FOR AGENCY FLEXIBILITY OR CONGRESSIONAL CONTROL

		Options increasing agency flexibility	**Options increasing congressional control**
	Key design questions		
Setting For further discussion of setting user fees, see GAO's Federal User Fees: A Design Guide, p. 7.a	**How are fee rates set?** Congress specifies how specific fee amounts will be determined. This could include specific dollar amounts, rates or other requirements	**By regulation** Congress may grant the agency the authority to set fee rates by following the rule-making process spelled out in the Administrative Procedure Act.	**In statute** Congress may set fee amounts or rates in statute.

		Options increasing agency flexibility	**Options increasing congressional control**
	Key design questions		
	(such as provisions for exemptions, waivers, and caps).		
Using For further discussion of using user fees, see GAO's Federal User Fees: A Design Guide, p. 26.[a]	**What Congressional action triggers the use of fee collections?** Collections are classified into 3 major categories: offsetting collections, offsetting receipts and governmental receipts.	**Offsetting collection authority** Offsetting collections are authorized by law to be credited to expenditure accounts from which they may be obligated without further legislation. However, an annual appropriation act may limit the total amount an agency may collect during a given fiscal year.	**Offsetting receipt authority** Government receipt authority Offsetting receipts and government receipts are required by law to be deposited into receipt accounts. Whether government receipts can be used without additional appropriation depends on the specific authorizing legislation for the collection. Offsetting receipt collections may not be used without additional appropriations.

Appendix I. (Continued)

		Options increasing agency flexibility	**Options increasing congressional control**
	Key design questions		
	What is the period of availability for the collections? Congress specifies the length of time for which collections are available for new obligations.	**No-year** No-year collections remain available for obligation for an indefinite period of time. A no-year appropriation of fee collections is usually identified by language such as "to remain available until expended."	**Limited year** One-year (fiscal year) or multiyear authority is available for a fixed period of time.
	For what purposes may the collections be used? Congress assigns the purpose(s) for which the collections can be used.	**Broadly defined uses** Congress may define the uses for particular collections broadly, for example, authorizing fees to be used for "all authorized activities and operations."	**Narrowly defined uses** Congress may define the uses for particular collections narrowly, authorizing fees to be used for specific, limited activities.
	To what degree will Congress limit the amount of collections that can be used? Congress sets the level of fee collections that the agency can spend in a given fiscal year.	**No limit** Congress may grant the agency the authority to spend all the money it collects without regard to amount or time.	**Limit set in statute** Congress may limit the amount of fee collections that the agency can spend to a particular dollar amount, often in

		Options increasing agency flexibility	**Options increasing congressional control**
	Key design questions		
			annual appropriations acts. In some cases, Congress sets the limit and provides specific direction for the treatment of collections in excess of that limit.
Reviewing For further discussion of reviewing user fees, see GAO's *Federal User Fees: A Design Guide, p. 33.*[a]	**What types of reporting and oversight requirements are in place?** Congress determines what type of requirements the agency must meet in order to permit the desired level of oversight.	**Basic requirements such as CFO Act Biennial Fee Reviews** Congress has designated basic review and reporting requirements. According to the CFO Act, the agency must review its fees on a biennial basis. This basic requirement applies for all 24 CFO Act agencies unless other requirements are specified for a particular fee program.	**Additional requirements** Congress may designate a number of additional requirements, such as reporting requirements and consulting with an advisory council. These requirements may be laid out in appropriations or authorizing legislation.

Source: GAO.

[a] GAO-08-386SP.

Appendix II: Key Questions about Costs and Collections to Enable Congress and Agencies to Identify and Manage Revenue Instability

What Data and Analysis Are Needed to Identify and Manage Revenue Instability?

- What is the risk that fee revenue instability will affect this program?
- What analysis should be performed and what data are needed?
- Are there limitations to the available data (such as preliminary estimates) that could add uncertainty to the collection estimates?
- How frequently should this analysis be conducted?

What Factors Could Affect the Timing and Pattern of Collections?

- How frequently are fees collected?
- What remittance compliance issues may exist, and what are the tools for ensuring compliance?
- What external known or unknown events could affect fee collections?
- How quickly is a change in collection amounts likely to occur?

What Factors Can Affect Costs in Fee-funded Programs?

- What are the fixed and variable costs of fee-funded activities?
- What is the timing and pattern of spending?
- Can the agency quickly respond to changing costs?
- What is the relationship between costs and revenue?

Closer Alignment of Fee Costs and Collections

- How quickly can the program adjust fee rates in response to changes in collections or costs?
- Are fees set at a rate that enables the program to respond to spikes or surges?
- Does the program have other sources of funding that may mitigate initial revenue shortfalls, or is the program fully fee-reliant?

Develop and Maintain a Reserve Fund

- What legal authority does the program or agency have to develop and fund a reserve?
- Does the agency need to notify Congress or seek permission, beyond its existing authority, to use its reserve fund?
- What is the goal of the reserve?
- Who should review and approve the reserve policy?
- What level of reserves should be maintained?
- How should the reserve fund be built and at what pace?

End Notes

[1] User charges from the public as reported in The President's Fiscal Year 2014 Budget Analytical Perspectives.

[2] We have also identified the key considerations for evaluating carryover balances in non-fee accounts. See GAO, Budget Issues: Key Questions to Consider When Evaluating Balances in Federal Accounts, GAO-13-798 (Washington, D.C.: Sept. 30, 2013).

[3] GAO, Federal User Fees: A Design Guide, GAO-08-386SP (Washington, D.C.: May 29, 2008).

[4] Chief Financial Officers Act of 1990, Pub. L. No. 101-576 (Nov. 15, 1990), codified at, 31 U.S.C. § 902.

[5] GAO, 2012 Annual Report: Opportunities to Reduce Duplication, Overlap and Fragmentation, Achieve Savings, and Enhance Revenue, GAO-12-342SP (Washington, D.C.: Feb. 28, 2012), 279-284.

[6] GAO-08-386SP.

[7] Without additional statutory authority to retain collections, fees collected under the IOAA are deposited in the general fund of the U.S. Treasury and are generally not available to the agency or the activity generating the fees. IOAA requires that agency regulations establishing a user fee are subject to policies prescribed by the President. OMB provides such guidance to executive branch agencies under this authority through OMB Circular No. A-25.

[8] Depending on the type of legislation providing the authority to collect or spend the fees, these funds are either mandatory or discretionary. Collections authorized in authorizing legislation are considered mandatory and collections that are authorized in appropriations legislation are discretionary.

[9] There are other Congressional design decisions that are not included in figure 1. These decisions have less direct bearing on the amount of agency flexibility or the nature of congressional control. For example, Congress could specify how an agency should collect its fees in some cases, but might delegate that decision to the agency in other cases. However, the Department of the Treasury established government-wide guidance directing agencies to use electronic collections in the absence of specific Congressional direction. As a result of this executive direction, even when Congress delegates the collection method to the agency, the implication for increased agency flexibility is generally less significant.

[10] The CFO Act requires agencies to review "fees, royalties, rents, and other charges imposed by the agency for services and things of value it provides." For the purposes of this discussion, GAO refers to all of these collectively as user fees.

[11] GAO, Federal User Fees: Additional Analyses and Timely Reviews Could Improve Immigration and Naturalization User Fee Design and USCIS Operations, GAO-09-180 (Washington, D.C.: Jan. 23, 2009).

[12] USCIS issued a subsequent fee review in 2010.

[13] In 2009 we found that USCIS's fees did not include the costs of certain retirement benefits paid by the Office of Personnel Management and the costs of the Department of Treasury's lockbox services—where some applications were received and processed. In response to our recommendation, USCIS identified these costs in its 2010 fee review. However, USCIS did not include these costs in setting its fees and the Office of Management and Budget concurred with USCIS's decision. See GAO, Immigration Applications Fees: Costing Methodology Improvements Would Provide More Reliable Basis for Setting Fees, GAO-09-70. (Washington, D.C.: Jan. 23, 2009).

[14] GAO, Patent and Trademark Office: New User Fee Design Presents Opportunities to Build on Transparency and Communication Success, GAO-12-514R (Washington, D.C.: Apr. 25, 2012).

[15] The use of fee waivers is one method of incorporating the ability-to-pay principle of equity in a fee design. See GAO-08-386SP and GAO-09-180.

[16] For examples, see GAO-08-386SP and GAO-12-514R.

[17] GAO-08-386SP.

[18] Federal Accounting Standards Advisory Board, Statement of Federal Financial Accounting Standards No. 4: Managerial Cost Accounting Standards and Concepts (July 31, 1995). Cost information can be used by Congress and federal executives in making decisions about allocating federal resources, authorizing and modifying programs, and evaluating program performance; it can also be used by program managers in making managerial decisions to improve operating economy and efficiency.

[19] The Budget Enforcement Act of 1990, defines offsetting collections and receipts as negative budget authority and the reductions to it as positive authority.

[20] GAO, Federal User Fees: Substantive Reviews Needed to Align Port-Related Fees with the Programs They Support, GAO-08-321 (Washington, D.C.: Feb. 22, 2008).

[21] GAO-08-321.

[22] GAO, Agricultural Quarantine Inspection Fees: Major Changes Needed to Align Fee Revenues with Program Costs, GAO-13-268 (Washington, D.C.: March 1, 2013).

[23] GAO-12-514R.

[24] Prior to enactment of the AIA, all fees collected were deposited into USPTO's account and were available to the extent appropriated. Since the enactment of AIA, collections during a fiscal year in excess of the amount appropriated to USPTO for the fiscal year are deposited into the new Patent and Trademark Fee Reserve Fund. As before, these excess collections are available to USPTO only to the extent appropriated by Congress. In 2012 we reported that the establishment of this special account increased transparency of these funds because any amounts appropriated, transferred, or rescinded from the fund would be clearly visible.

[25] As of July 2013, this backlog has been reduced to approximately 591,000 patent applications.

[26] Pub. L. No. 82-137 (Aug. 31, 1951), codified at, 31 U.S.C. § 9701.

[27] Specifically, 21 of the 23 agencies that responded to our survey reported varying levels of adherence to the biennial review and reporting requirements. The survey responses

indicated that for most fees, agencies (1) had not discussed fee review results in annual reports, and (2) had not reviewed the fees and were inconsistent in their ability to provide fee review documentation. The 24th CFO Act agency, the Department of Defense, did not respond to our survey in time to be included. See GAO, 2012 Annual Report: Opportunities to Reduce Duplication, Overlap and Fragmentation, Achieve Savings, and Enhance Revenue, GAO-12-342SP (Washington, D.C.: Feb. 28, 2012).

[28] GAO, "General Government: Federal User Fees," GAO's Action Tracker (Washington, DC: March 6, 2013), accessed July 25, 2013, http://www.gao.gov/duplication/action_tracker/Federal_User_Fees/action1.

[29] GAO-09-180. For example, in 2007 we found that under CBP's authorizing statute for passenger inspection user fees, not all activities that may be funded from the customs fee were necessarily associated with conducting air passenger inspections, and not all inspection activities were reimbursable by funds from the user fee account. We concluded in that report that unless agencies present a comprehensive picture of the fees, including the full scope of inspection activities and their costs, Congress will lack a complete picture of whether the fees work in concert or conflict with each other, which could hamper oversight. See GAO, Federal User Fees: Key Aspects of International Air Passenger Inspection Fees Should be Addressed Regardless of Whether Fees are Consolidated, GAO-07-1131 (Washington, D.C.: Sept. 24, 2007).

[30] GAO-08-321 and GAO-07-1131.

[31] GAO-08-386SP.

[32] Congress passed legislation in late 2010 that included a number of supplemental appropriations and rescissions affecting various government agencies. Included among them was a $120 million supplemental appropriation for USPTO. As a result of this supplemental appropriation, USPTO had access to almost all fees collected during fiscal year 2010

[33] The AIA created a second account, the Patent and Trademark Fee Reserve Fund. USPTO collections in excess of appropriations are to be deposited into this account. In the fiscal year 2012 appropriations, Congress provided USPTO with access to the funds in the Patent and Fee Trademark Reserve Fund; this was extended through FY 2013 by the continuing resolution. However, according to USPTO officials, there is currently no balance in the Reserve Fund.

[34] We recommended in April 2012 that USPTO finalize an operating reserve policy, including the expected level of reserves, to smooth the impact of economic downturns on operations and to ensure its use aligns with agency goals. The Department of Commerce accepted this recommendation. See GAO, Patent and Trademark Office: New User Fee Design Presents Opportunities to Build on Transparency and Communication Success, GAO-12-514R (Washington, D.C.: Apr. 12, 2012).

[35] USF collections are administered by the USAC, which is a non-governmental, private entity. As such, USF contributions are not subject to the appropriations process, unlike FCC's regulatory fee collections held in the agency's salaries and expenses account.

[36] In August 2012, we recommended that Congress should consider whether FCC's excess regulatory fees (approximately $66 million through fiscal year 2011) should be appropriated for FCC's use, or, if not, what the disposition of these funds should be, and whether to change FCC's annual appropriations language to permit reconciliation of excess collections or to govern FCC's handling of any future excess collections. Congress has not as yet taken any action. See GAO, Federal Communications Commission: Regulatory Process Needs to Be Updated, GAO-12-686, (Washington, D.C.: Aug. 10, 2012), 36.

[37] USF contributions are paid monthly by telecommunications carriers (including landline and wireless companies, interconnected Voice over Internet Protocol (VoIP) providers, and other providers of telecommunications) based on their projected revenues. The contributions are collected by the Universal Service Administrative Company (USAC) an independent, not-for-profit corporation created in 1997 to collect universal service contributions and administer universal support programs.

[38] GAO, Telecommunications: FCC Has Reformed the High-Cost Program, but Oversight and Management Could Be Improved, GAO-12-738 (Washington, D.C.: July 25, 2012.); Telecommunications: FCC's Performance Management Weaknesses Could Jeopardize Proposed Reforms of the Rural Health Care Program, GAO-11-27 (Washington, D.C.: Nov. 17, 2010); Telecommunications: Improved Management Can Enhance FCC Decision Making for the Universal Service Fund Low-Income Program, GAO-11-11 (Washington, D.C.: Oct. 28, 2010); Telecommunications: FCC Should Assess the Design of the E-rate Program's Internal Control Structure, GAO-10-908 (Washington, D.C.: Sept. 29, 2010).

[39] Ensuring that fees are set at a rate to cover the intended costs is referred to as revenue adequacy. We discuss the key considerations for ensuring revenue adequacy in GAO-08-386SP.

[40] Programs that rely solely on general fund appropriations can also experience fluctuations in funding, but the causes and considerations are distinct from those affecting fee-reliant programs.

[41] See GAO-08-386SP for the questions to consider when designing and implementing user fees.

[42] GAO, Internal Controls: Standards for Internal Controls in the Federal Government, GAO/AIMD-00-21.3.1. (Washington, D.C.: November, 1999.)

[43] GAO-13-268.

[44] GAO-09-180.

[45] GAO-13-268. In 2013, we recommended that the Secretary of Homeland Security establish internal controls to alert personnel when fees are not paid, and to use available information to verify that arriving trucks, private aircraft, and private vessels pay applicable inspection user fees.

[46] Penalties need to be strong enough to deter unwanted behavior but not so severe that they cannot practically be imposed. For more information on design of non-remittance penalties, see GAO-07-1131.

[47] GAO, Telecommunications: Improved Management Can Enhance FCC Decision Making for the Universal Service Fund Low-Income Program, GAO-11-11 (Washington, D.C.: Oct. 28, 2010).

[48] Since the release of our 2010 report, the FCC made efforts to address the risks of telecommunication providers' inconsistent adherence to applicant eligibility requirements. For example, the Lifeline Reform Order established uniform eligibility criteria for the federal Lifeline program, and required service providers to determine whether a subscriber was in fact eligible for Lifeline service, based on documentation provided by the subscriber, rather than allowing subscribers to self-certify their eligibility. See Lifeline and Link Up Reform and Modernization et al., WC Docket Nos. 11-42 et al., Report and Order and Further Notice of Proposed Rulemaking, 27 FCC Rcd 6656 (2012) (Lifeline Reform Order).

[49] See GAO-08-386SP for more information about price elasticity and fee-funded programs.

[50] Funding USCIS' information technology investments with premium-processing fees was consistent with Congressional report language accompanying the fiscal years 2008-2010 Department of Homeland Security appropriations bills.

[51] In December 2000, Congress authorized the collection of a premium processing fee in addition to the regular application fees for employment-based applications. Congress set the amount of the fee at $1,000 and directed that these amounts be available for (1) the premium processing activities and (2) infrastructure improvements associated with adjudications and customer-service.

[52] GAO, Budget Issues: Better Fee Design Would Improve Federal Protective Service's and Federal Agencies' Planning and Budgeting for Security, GAO-11-492 (Washington, DC: May 20, 2011).

INDEX

#

A

B

C

D

G

H

I

J

L

M

N

O

P

V

W